KU-511-385

62
.BAD

Overseas Research

Social Science Library
Oxford University Library Services
Manor Road
Oxford OX1 3UQ

A
Practical
Guide

Overseas Research

CHRISTOPHER B. BARRETT
AND JEFFREY W. CASON

THE JOHNS HOPKINS UNIVERSITY PRESS
BALTIMORE AND LONDON

© 1997 The Johns Hopkins University Press
All rights reserved. Published 1997
Printed in the United States of America on acid-free paper

06 05 04 03 02 01 00 99 98 97   5 4 3 2 1

The Johns Hopkins University Press
2715 North Charles Street
Baltimore, Maryland 21218-4319
The Johns Hopkins Press Ltd., London

A catalog record for this book is available from the British Library.

LIBRARY OF CONGRESS CATALOGING-IN-PUBLICATION DATA

Barrett, Christopher B. (Christopher Brendan)
   Overseas research : a practical guide / Christopher B. Barrett and Jeffrey W.
   Cason.
      p.   cm.
   Includes bibliographical references and index.
   ISBN 0-8018-5513-6 (hc : alk. paper). — ISBN 0-8018-5514-4 (pbk. : alk. paper)
   1. Social sciences—Field work.   I. Cason, Jeffrey W.   II. Title.
   H62.B338   1997
   300'.7'23—dc21   96-48307

Contents

Field Narratives

Foreword

This book came out of a project to test whether knowledge and perspectives from countries outside the United States can contribute to deeper understanding of regional security dilemmas and strategies for international cooperation. With financial support from the John D. and Catherine T. MacArthur Foundation, junior and senior scholars from the University of Wisconsin–Madison created an interdisciplinary learning community. Faculty and students took up the challenge of interdisciplinary training and research in peace and international cooperation with unusual energy and commitment.

At least two assumptions guided the effort. First, to investigate the dynamics of conflict and cooperation in civil or regional conflicts, we need a range of disciplinary tools. Economic, social, cultural, and technological factors, among others, contribute to conflict, so people trained in corresponding disciplines can offer useful methods of investigating these complex social processes. Second, students and young professionals bring fresh approaches and important, if sometimes uncomfortable, questions to the study of regional conflicts and global trends; they can challenge conventional wisdom and stimulate new understanding.

While we all expected that graduate students' research and field experiences would be enriched by the project, none of us could have anticipated the book that Christopher Barrett and Jeffrey Cason have authored. Drawing on field research experiences of students at the University of Wisconsin and of those supported by the Ford Foundation through the Social Science Research Council's International Predissertation Fellowship Program, this book provides valuable guidance for those heading to the field for the first time.

The authors address that gray area of research experience between participation and observation. Anyone who has been immersed in a new culture to learn about the complex patterns of interaction is familiar with the tension between the roles of observer and participant. Important insights can be gained through direct observation as a participant in a foreign setting. And for many researchers, participant observation in the field forms the basis of a lifelong commitment to research in a particular country or region beyond their own. Successfully straddling the line between participant and observer may be the single most important skill students can obtain in the course of dissertation field research. As Barrett and Cason suggest, "Fieldwork is a sequence of decision, some about the conduct of research, some about the conduct of life." It is at the intersection of conducting research and living life that some of the most penetrating insights may come. This book will help focus researchers' attention on that productive intersection.

This collection of experiences will also prepare first-time field researchers in practical ways for what is always an unnerving, messy, and difficult time. Such preparation is particularly important in an era of reduced funding for field research in social sciences. The steady erosion of financial resources for overseas travel, scholarly exchanges, and social science research are taking their toll on the opportunities for direct field experience in societies outside the United States. Because of limited funding, it is incumbent on those who are able to obtain money to travel, study, and live abroad to use it carefully and wisely. Scholars no longer have the luxury of spending precious time "reinventing the wheel" to do effective field research. That is another reason that *Overseas Research* should prove to be an important contribution; it can prepare young fieldworkers in the practical, logistical, and psychological considerations of very demanding work, help save valuable time, and make the most of scarce financial resources.

This publication grew out of the experiences of many individuals, financially supported by a range of private philanthropic and public governmental sources. Without the initiative of the students and the intellectual guidance of faculty and administrators at the University of Wisconsin, however, the knitting together of these experiences in a community of learning would not have happened. The practice of students mentoring other students is not new, but the extent to which the Wisconsin program encouraged a self-conscious and open sharing of information and experience is unusual. Hopefully, this initiative will inspire others to contribute, even at a time of declining resources, to cooperative and effective training in international social sciences.

Kennette Benedict, Director
Program on Peace and International Cooperation
John D. and Catherine T. MacArthur Foundation

Preface and Acknowledgments

It is customary to begin a preface by acknowledging how the final product would have been impossible without the help of many others. As the reader will soon discover, this book is exceptional in the degree to which direct and concrete assistance was provided by many individuals. Indeed, the project would have been infeasible without others' quite active participation. Those listed as contributors provided detailed responses to a questionnaire distributed by the coauthors, and many took time to review and correct a draft manuscript. We thank them for their time and thoughtfulness. In addition, many fellows in the Social Science Research Council's International Predissertation Fellowship Program released copies of reports on their fieldwork to us. We thank the following individuals for such cooperation: Regina Abrami, Robert Andolina, Sarah Babb, Clifford Bob, Charla Britt, Cameron Campbell, Karen Sue Crehore, Thamora Fishel, Leslie Gray, Janice Harper, Stephen Herschler, William Kandel, Stephen Kay, Morgan Yih-Yang Liu, Steve Marquardt, Ann Marie Murphy, Albert Park, Janet Roitman, Marc Stern, Keiko Tanaka, Twila Tardif, Margaret Weigers, Jurgen Wiesmann, and Chris Woodruff. Some other SSRC Predisseration fellows also responded to the questionnaire; they are listed with the contributors. We thank Ellen Perecman and Amy Chazkel of the SSRC for facilitating this cooperation and for their enthusiastic support. Richard Lobban and Leonardo Villalón kindly shared materials from a panel on research issues in West Africa they convened at the November 1994 annual meeting of the African Studies Association in Toronto. In addition to those who contributed with their fieldwork experience, Patricia Gray and Jon Moris provided substantial suggestions, especially for the bibliography.

The idea for the book grew out of the MacArthur/SSRC scholars program at the University of Wisconsin–Madison, housed within the Global Studies Research Program (GSRP). We thank Michael Carter, Jim Riker, and Barbara Stallings for their facilitation and support of this progam. We especially thank David Trubek for providing the resources and moral support to turn our proposal into a project, and Carol Torgeson for outstanding administrative support. Laurie Brown, Sandy Lee, and especially Ruby Vazquez of the Economics Department at Utah State were unceasingly helpful and patient in preparing the manuscript, and Mary Duffy provided help on a moment's notice on the Vermont end of the project. In addition, the MacArthur Foundation's support for the consortium between the University of Wisconsin, the University of Minnesota, and Stanford University provided additional contributors, and the consortium's June 1995 Summer Institute in Madison provided a wonderful opportunity to present the first draft of the manuscript for comments and suggestions. We thank Kennette Benedict of the MacArthur Foundation for her support of the consortium's activities. The skilled staff at the Johns Hopkins University Press have made the publication process uncommonly pleasant. We especially thank Henry Tom, Miriam Tillman, and Hilary Reeves for the care they have given our work.

Finally, our families deserve credit, thanks, and gratitude for supporting our own fieldwork and putting up with the time demands of this book. It is an understatement to say they have been an inspiration and support. Brendan and Mary Catherine tolerated their father's extended absences and, along with Joanna, the rigors of writing. Through it all and over exceptionally long distances, Clara has made Chris's international work possible and worthwhile. Although vicarious, her field experiences have been no less arduous and invigorating than Chris's. Carolina Menéndez has come to the field with Jeff on several occasions and provided concrete help in the research process. More important—and this became particularly obvious when the field was faced alone—she provided the companionship that made living in the field a joy. Carolina also provided a quite tangible contribution to this book, as she compiled the index. For these reasons and many others, we dedicate this book to Clara and Carolina.

Overseas Research

1

Introduction

Every year a great number of enthusiastic, well-trained social scientists set out on their first overseas research project and, with an awesome display of energy and creativity, reinvent the flat tire. To some extent their difficulties are inevitable. Moreover, the war stories we all bring back from the field often add zest to the rigors of scholarly research. Yet it is too often equally true that projects drag on needlessly, data sets become corrupted, scarce funds are squandered, and researchers get demoralized by missteps and obstacles that might have been avoided.

We believe that a fair proportion of such missteps and obstacles are due not to poor formal training, but to a lack of field-tested advice on practical matters. Any social scientist who has set out to collect data in "the field" knows the gnawing feeling that previous methodological study is of limited value in the successful conduct of field research. When such research is conducted in a foreign culture, the doubts and worries inevitably multiply. What a researcher often yearns for is something between a technical manual on data collection and a chatty travel guide. This book aims to begin to fill that void.

We have gathered information and experiences gleaned from more than a hundred scholar-years of overseas fieldwork, reported directly to us or to funding agencies (when scholars authorized release of the relevant reports). As one fellow wrote to the Social Science Research Council (SSRC), "There is a large amount of information available on practical and academic issues that grad students frequently face when heading to the field. The problem is that this information is scattered and difficult to obtain." It is our hope that this volume makes it easier to gain access to a large portion of such information.

We qualify our ambitions, however, by recognizing that familiarity with the research site is an important and highly idiosyncratic part of mastering the field methods relevant to any particular project. Still, there are cautions, techniques, and tips that have demonstrated wide applicability across disciplines and continents. We pull many such threads together here in hopes of alleviating some of the stress felt by overseas researchers, especially social scientists on their first major research project, and of thereby helping improve the quality of social science research. Our dream is that copies of this book will have dog-eared pages stained with airline coffee and covers worn from frequent rubbing against the rucksack frames of researchers who become avid and productive observers of the diverse societies that span the globe.

Much of what this book covers falls under the heading of common sense: learning where you are and about the people with whom you live and work, thinking through the ramifications of your words and deeds, anticipating and preparing for contingencies. With the exception of exploring means of dealing with particular problems that might be faced in executing a research plan (Chapter 6), we avoid technical issues of research methodology (e.g., sampling, questionnaire design, interviewing technique) for three reasons. First, disciplinary courses thoroughly cover both theoretical issues that motivate fieldwork and methodological issues that exploit the data collected; and the chasm between hypothesis and test is bridged formally by a substantial research methods literature. Second, most scholars at the doctoral level remain pious about disciplinary traditions, and integrating these disparate approaches far exceeds our abilities. Third, it is not altogether clear that most of a field researcher's time is really spent on research. In a perhaps exaggerated claim, Nigel Barley says that scarcely 1 percent of his time in Cameroon was spent conducting research, with 99 percent dedicated to "logistics, being ill, being sociable, arranging things, getting from place to place, and above all, waiting" (Barley 1983, 98). Even for those graced with an abundance of pure research time in the field, mundane activities merit attention in their own right. Yet neither disciplinary courses nor academic advisers nor the published literature meet the palpable need of inexperienced researchers for current, field-tested advice on practical issues of planning, preparing, and conducting fieldwork.

We hypothesize that young scholars mentored in mundane matters have more enjoyable and productive research experiences. This belief is born of our own experiences in the MacArthur Scholars Program at the University of Wisconsin–Madison. Wisconsin's MacArthur scholars enjoy unusually fertile cross-disciplinary sharing of perspectives on theory, methods, and, especially, the day-to-day details of international social science research through formal workshops, less formal round tables, and informal social gatherings. By sharing practical insights gleaned from their own research experiences, scholars already returned from the field routinely aid newer scholars in the design, preparation, and execution of successful projects. Although it is impossible to establish how much value this environment has added to the research of a select group of capable and energetic young scholars, the cumulative results suggest that the whole has exceeded the sum of its parts.

In researching this book we surveyed approximately 150 scholars funded in the past six years by the MacArthur Scholars programs at Stanford and Wisconsin or the Social Science Research Council's International Predissertation Fellowship Program. Including a few others who volunteered their experiences, we received responses from sixty-three social scientists representing eight disciplines at twenty universities. Collectively the respondents undertook extensive field research in forty-three countries in Africa, Asia, the Caribbean, Europe, Latin America, and the Middle East. This group's experience in funding overseas research was outstanding. Virtually all received funding from major research programs, such as Fulbright or Fulbright-Hays, the Inter-American Foundation, the Institute for the Study of World Politics, the Midwestern Universities Consortium for International Activities, the National Science Foundation, the Rockefeller Foundation, the Social Science Research Council, the Tinker Foundation, Wenner-Gren, or the West Africa Research Association. Moreover, these research projects have borne scholarly fruit. In less than five years, these research projects have already generated several dozen scholarly journal articles and book chapters, as well as several books and dissertation awards. Most members of the group have now completed their doctorates and taken up positions at major research universities, leading liberal arts colleges, or international or nongovernmental organizations. A sizable majority continue active international research. The impressive collective record of the graduate students involved in these programs likely owes something to the opportunities presented for informal and formal sharing of insights on how to design, execute, and survive overseas research projects. This book is an attempt to share those fruits with a broader audience in similar circumstances.

It is essential, for at least two reasons, that the reader keep in mind that this volume is a compilation of many scholars' lessons learned from overseas field research. First, this is no cookbook; not all points are relevant or appropriate to all research settings. We aim to jog the memory, good judgment, and conscience of overburdened field researchers, not to substitute for those resources. Second, we do not want the mass of detail that follows to intimidate or discourage anyone, especially not newcomers to the field. Just as no one scholar alone could have offered these insights, so too it is unlikely that any single person could follow completely the guidelines offered in this volume. Read and digest it in bits, as needed, with the full appreciation that all the contributors themselves have to some degree stumbled through fieldwork but ultimately emerged the better for the experience(s).

The two of us, although experienced, are not experts at fieldwork; we serve mainly as rapporteurs for a successful group. We compiled the volume iteratively. First, we solicited comments using a detailed outline of open-ended questions corresponding to the book's structure and encouraged respondents to add their own questions. The cooperating scholars thereby defined the book's content, if not entirely its structure. Many also released to us copies of related reports they had filed with grantsmaking organizations. We then drafted the volume, relying extensively on scholars' solicited and unsolicited responses, and recirculated the full text to those researchers, as well as to external reviewers, for correction, enhancement, and refinement. This second round of comments guided final revisions. We quote directly and liberally from contributed remarks, both to represent experiences accurately and to provide a sense of the group's wide-ranging (sometimes conflicting) lessons learned.

We decided against an edited volume so as to maximize the integration of related insights and to minimize redundancy. Perhaps, more important, synthesis facilitated structuring the presentation to correspond to the chronology of an overseas research project: beginning with site selection and funding, continuing through predeparture preparations, field activities, and repatriation, and ending with considerations that endure long after the return from the field. Fieldwork is a sequence of decisions, some about the conduct of research, some about the conduct of life. This volume presents many decisions commonly faced by social scientists overseas, roughly in the order in which they arise. We provide some guidance on how others have resolved such decisions, both satisfactorily and unsatisfactorily. The basic approach is thus to identify prospective decisions, map out common alternatives, and, where the evidence and logic are strong, proffer prescriptions.

It should be evident that one cannot divorce the practice of data collection from the physical and social environment within which data are collected. For that reason, interpenetrating professional and personal matters are addressed together throughout the volume. This process involves not only the management of time, talents, and resources but also some of the difficult ethical choices researchers must routinely make. Overseas research (especially in low-income societies), which regularly places northern elite fieldworkers among sometimes desperately poor people in alien cultures, frequently elicits profound experiences in which issues of personal conduct can be of singular importance.

We do not pretend to have run perfect research projects. Indeed, some of this volume's most valuable offerings derive from costly and embarrassing failures. Nor do we claim to have all the questions, much less the answers, concerning practical matters of overseas research. After all, there are ever new developments, and there is no substitute for exercising good judgment. Yet we believe good judgment can be honed by anticipating and reviewing prospective challenges and decisions, some of which are identifiable from the past experiences of other researchers. This book should help in that endeavor. Field research is not deterministically controlled by an investigator—that not only would prove dull, but would likely suffocate illuminating discoveries born of chance—but neither is it a fatalistic endeavor. One exerts considerable influence over one's research environment by the resolution of particular issues that frequently arise. In the eight chapters that follow we present a compendium of one group's guidance on many such issues that comprise the potentially marvelous experience of overseas fieldwork.

2

Identifying a Site and Funding Source

Fieldwork begins at home, and the portion done at home is often no less taxing than that accomplished abroad. Indeed, many scholars find the first step in a research project the hardest. The initial challenges, sometimes daunting, that we explore in this chapter include selecting a site and funding a project. We identify the issues to consider in the earliest stages of defining and funding an overseas research project. In identifying these issues, we describe some common obstacles you can expect and suggest how to navigate successfully around them.

With the important exceptions of research projects that are subsumed within a larger research program and evaluations of specific events or projects, the process of selecting a site generally precedes courting funding agencies.

Site Selection

It is perhaps obvious that you need to have a research site before conducting overseas field research. After hypotheses are preliminarily defined, you must decide where, when, and how to investigate the question(s) at hand. This can be a difficult enterprise as you try to balance personal and professional objectives, often in a state of extreme ignorance. The "homemade" decisions that result substantially influence the course of subsequent fieldwork and, thus, are not to be taken lightly.

Certainly, sites must be chosen because the *place* interests you.

However, you must also consider the feasibility and future market-ability of the research project as well as personal and family needs or preferences. In addition, timing can play a critical role. Obviously, the appropriate weighing of alternative professional and personal criteria depends on a wide variety of individual circumstances.

The appropriate balance among these criteria does, nonetheless, vary somewhat predictably across disciplines and methods. For instance, researchers fielding a formal survey and aspiring to quantitative data analysis leading to general policy implications typically need to give more attention to how the location or timing of research might affect sample frame construction or respondent participation rates. On the other hand, researchers who are undertaking a qualitative ethnography—where they are likely to be in the field for an extended period—may be less concerned with the precise timing of the research. In some cases, once you decide upon a topic and country for research, the site becomes obvious. A scholar studying decision-making within the central state bureaucracy almost inevitably must locate in the national capital. A researcher studying a particular sort of economic or cultural activity must obviously go to where such activities are prominent. Historians generally must go to wherever the appropriate documents are archived.

But sometimes site selection is far from obvious. One of the coauthor's work on the effects of economic liberalization on rural food marketing and production could have been conducted in any of thousands of towns and villages in a host of countries. Especially when the physical location of an appropriate site is relatively unimportant, considerations of timing, feasibility, marketability, and personal preferences weigh heavily in the final choice of a research site.

There are a multitude of temporal issues to consider in site selection. Those doing rural research must pay attention to agricultural calendars, which dictate seasonal labor, migration, and expenditure patterns. Rainy seasons can seriously disrupt travel or necessitate extra expenditures for an appropriate vehicle. Political or cultural events, such as electoral campaigns or uncommon festivals, can heavily influence the environment in which you collect data. The month around or following Christmas is "down time" in many Christian cultures. In Islamic cultures, the month of Ramadan can accelerate a respondent's fatigue in daytime interviewing, forcing much research into hours of darkness. It is important to identify local holidays and vacation periods in establishing your fieldwork schedule.

Young scholars often overlook the crucial timing issue of sequencing fieldwork and preparatory literature review at the home institution. Anxious to get to the field, many do not leave sufficient time to prepare at home before departing overseas. Although it may appear obvious, many researchers learn the hard way the value of a complete and careful reading of the relevant empirical and theoretical literature available at the home institution before departure. This saves valuable field time otherwise spent collecting superfluous secondary materials or trying to pin down the research question. One researcher left for the field only one day after completing his Ph.D. preliminary examinations, having done only a skimpy literature review, and ended up with disastrous results. He reported that as a consequence, "I had only a superficial understanding of the place, and I wasted enormous amounts of time and effort collecting materials that were indeed available at home. This also had a very negative impact on my ability to narrow my research topic. As a result, I consider this to have been my greatest mistake, and if there is anything I will make sure to do in the future, it will be to avoid a repetition of this experience." Greg White echoes this point in the narrative below.

Another scholar, who did take time to prepare well in advance of his departure, emphasized the "key importance of adequate prior training in field techniques," which can be central to establishing the feasibility of the initial research design and adapting it accordingly. Others noted that an examination of past dissertations based on re-

---

The Value of Preparing at Home

You can't underestimate the value of being thoroughly familiar with the resources available at your home institution. Furthermore, with the advent of the internet, one is increasingly able to map what's available in the field. I was in the field for the first time in 1990, essentially the pre-internet era, and I was convinced that my home university's library would not have volumes from the early 1970s of the superb *Annuaire de l'Afrique du Nord*. As a result, I spent hours poring over the volumes in the archives in Tunisia and France. Of course, I "wept" when I returned to Madison and found that the library did, indeed, have a full complement of volumes.

GREG WHITE

search in the targeted country can provide valuable leads to data sources as well as obscure but useful archival materials.

In general, the more empirical the nature of a research project, the more focused site selection tends to be at the outset, thus making the research task simpler. Yet researchers with such an early, clear vision of where they will do fieldwork may start off with an insufficient theoretical framework, which can lead to aimless empiricism and frustration. As a corollary, the more theoretical the issues to be investigated, the less precise the researcher's initial thoughts about an appropriate site, thus making site selection more challenging. For scholars of this stripe, a preliminary visit to the field is especially valuable. (We address exploratory research trips in the next section.)

This brings us naturally to considerations regarding the broader aims of the study, that is, to the desired degree of specificity of the research project, which is often correlated with its empirical or theoretical roots. Prior research about the selected area can be of enormous value, providing baseline data or, in the best of cases, a foundation for constructing a longitudinal study. One anthropologist was pleased to find that "the ethnohistoric and ethnographic record for [his] area [was] sound, allowing the insertion of [his] research interests into a broader analytical map." Preexisting primary data sets likewise influenced site selection for a number of other, especially quantitatively oriented, researchers.

The feasibility of the project must be established clearly and early along at least two dimensions. First, is the prospective research site relevant to the hypotheses you wish to test? Can you get sufficient variation along a number of different axes to control for confounding variables and isolate the relationships of interest? Do you have the necessary language skills to survive and to fulfill the research objectives in the research site? (We will address language and language training later in this chapter.) Second, can the research design be implemented logistically and administratively in the proposed site? If interregional (much less international) communications or transport are important, can the infrastructure support project requirements? Simple issues, like the existence of appropriate scale maps or electricity, can matter enormously to the feasibility of a particular research design. Administratively and intellectually, it is often advantageous to have a host country collaborator, so you will want to consider identifying indigenous researchers conducting similar work.

A central issue of feasibility concerns the acceptability of the research topic to a host government, should the research require clearance. One scholar reported to the Social Science Research Council (SSRC) on his return from an exploratory research trip, "I am more acutely aware of the . . . government's sensitivity to the issues I had planned to examine and of the difficulties of carrying out research that is not to the government's liking." It became plain to this individual that his "original research plans would not be feasible without extensive and risky subterfuge," and he subsequently adjusted the research topic and design.

As a researcher, your nationality influences the feasibility of a given project. "Insider" researchers (i.e., host country natives) often have more extensive contacts and multiple means of satisfying logistical needs. In particular, nationals of the host country generally meet less resistance in securing research clearance on potentially inflammatory subjects than do foreigners, whom the government might consider insensitive to the social and political environment. Razavi (1993) made this case strongly in describing her research in Iran. Your gender can be a factor as well. Several women reported sensing they had an easier time negotiating bureaucratic obstacles, albeit for the unfortunate reason that many governments do not take female researchers seriously enough to consider them a potential threat.

Having raised the issue of insider research, we should note it often carries less status professionally. Many grantsmakers will not fund research in the country of origin or in peripheral communities within the United States or its territories. Furthermore, some potential employers, especially academic departments, look down upon those who return to their native lands for research as if they somehow lacked the courage to step away from the familiar. In doing so, they ignore the fact that familiarity can be a valuable asset in research.

Indeed, the future marketability of research almost invariably figures prominently in site selection, if only subconsciously. Francisca James-Hernandez makes this claim eloquently in the narrative opposite. Advisers and colleagues invariably recommend sites for their "policy relevance," prestige, or potential to publish the results obtained there. Young social scientists almost invariably, and probably wisely, tend to heed such advice.

As Hernandez notes, "passion" is a powerful attractor (or repellent) in site selection. This accounts in part for the common phenomenon of overseas volunteers (e.g., Peace Corps) returning later as scientists on a research project. Personal and family concerns are undoubtedly the most understated determinants of research location and timing. This is probably because scientists are reluctant to acknowledge anything other than scientific bases for site selection. Nonetheless, such concerns exert enormous influence over the ultimate choice, and properly so. Heading to the field with a pregnant wife or a husband not quite finished with his degree is hard on everyone. Taking small children to malaria- and plague-infested areas borders on recklessness,

---

Choosing the Research Site

Consciously or not, I submit most researchers consider status in choosing their research topic, field site, theoretical orientation, and the population studied. I suspect most deny it, however, believing academe is fundamentally meritocratic, functioning on the free trade of ideas. Even so, it's only realistic and pragmatic to be aware of how ideas are rated better or worse in the intellectual marketplace. The choice of field site and others made throughout the research process have an impact on the possibilities of getting an attentive or knowledgeable academic adviser (if you're a student), getting published (including access to publishers), getting academic appointments, getting grants, getting tenure, and so on. All of these and other considerations are the cultural capital of the field. This said, I don't advocate a choice of field site based exclusively on maximum career returns. High cultural capital can be deceptive and is not necessarily nurturing of one's intellectual creativity nor of that intangible rarely acknowledged in academe, one's happiness.

In my view, the choice of field site is, ideally, one of passion. Where do you feel most passionate as a researcher? What place gets you excited, warms your cheeks at the thought, and, above all, inspires you to write? What place and population will get you through months of 100-degrees-plus weather, intestinal parasites, sexual assaults, tarantulas for the arachnophobic, or whatever else it is that will make fieldwork precarious, dangerous, boring, frightening, enraging, stupefying, or any of the other potential myriad obstacles that will, inevitably, arise from time to time, if not constantly?

FRANCISCA JAMES-HERNANDEZ

and living in a polluted and perhaps hostile city has its own problems. Evacuation tends to be simpler and quicker for a single adult than for a family in a research area subject to civil strife. Personal and professional concerns are difficult to disentangle. Personal misery or stress too often ruins the research experience, while a joyful personal experience often contributes to outstanding fieldwork, if only invisibly.

Many researchers reported that their choice of sites was initially guided by personal interests, and only the refinement of site selection was determined by "professional" criteria. The choice of country in which to undertake fieldwork is commonly influenced by dependents' language skills, professional situation, and life style. Indeed, one researcher remarked, only partly in jest, that "the only valid criteria for choosing [sites] are an abiding fondness for the food, music, and people!" Conversely, several people reported not choosing prospective sites because of serious concerns about health conditions, security, or the availability of activities to engage accompanying dependents.

Researchers with families understandably place a great premium on finding a place where their dependents can be happy. For some, happiness is equated with North American conveniences, thereby sharply narrowing the range of prospective field sites. One contributor who took a wife and child to the field freely admitted that, in site selection, "my real reasons were personal, but academic theoretical reasoning matched my practical needs perfectly—a rare stroke of luck." We suspect his site selection process to be far more common than most researchers publicly acknowledge.

That said, some disciplined souls swallow hard and, despite knowing the difficulties of a site, consciously choose it anyway because of its outstanding research attributes. Some reported that it took a year or more to acclimate to the discomforts of living in, as one researcher described it, "a sort of equatorial hell, a malaria-infested lowland farming center that had been destroyed in the war and then left forgotten for a decade and a half." In our observation, unaccompanied fieldworkers are by far most likely to exhibit the grit necessary to make such a choice.

Exploratory Research Trips

The problem of site selection has multiple levels. Once you have decided on a country in which to do your research, the choice of the particular city, region, and subpopulation are still before you. An ex-

ploratory trip can help enormously in pinning down a site by permitting the selection process to be subdivided into stages. In the first
stage, you can consider the broad questions of topic, general timing,
and host country (or a small set of contiguous alternatives) at your
home institution. But if given the chance to make a preparatory visit
to the host country, you can put off the particulars of location and timing (which are influenced by issues of feasibility and personal needs,
resources, and preferences) until learning more about the alternatives
firsthand.

Thus, the best recommendation we can offer is, when at all possible, do exploratory research before making a longer-term commitment. Indeed, those researchers we consulted considered this such a
crucial part of a good research plan that several recommended funding this initial trip as an out-of-pocket expense, if necessary. Consider
it an investment bearing handsome dividends. Several weeks spent in
the field at this stage can save several months of frustration later on.
Moreover, grantsmaking organizations generally look favorably upon
in-country experience, established collaborative affiliations, and the
clearer sense of understanding of the important questions and feasible
research designs that come from an exploratory research visit.

Thankfully, there are means by which a young scholar can finance
exploratory research trips without resorting to credit card stress. The
SSRC introduced an International Predissertation Fellowship Program (IPFP) in 1990, the intent of which is to facilitate the development of feasible empirical dissertation projects through exploratory
field research. Many of the researchers we consulted for this volume
benefited from the IPFP. In addition, most major research universities
and many Title VI area studies programs in the United States have
regular competitions for small travel grants, which are designed to
provide seed money toward more substantial extramural funding.
Those involved in overseas consulting may have the opportunity to
reroute flights through a potential research locale and to take a few
weeks to scout out the site and, thus, gather necessary materials, determine the feasibility and appropriateness of the research, and establish the necessary contacts. Two researchers did this quite successfully, "dropping by" Ethiopia and Togo on the way back to the
U.S. from Zimbabwe and Morocco, respectively.

An exploratory research trip of a few months (although even just
several weeks may suffice) permits you to establish contacts and lo-

cate potential collaborators; to find institutions with which you might wish to affiliate; to dig through the archives, literature, and data already available in-country; and to investigate living conditions. You can then return home to revisit the relevant empirical and theoretical literature and to investigate subjects previously overlooked but revealed by the light of the recent trip to the field.

An exploratory visit inevitably builds contacts that prove useful later on. For example, one of the coauthors was able to line up enumerator teams for interviews and training before returning to the field because a preparatory visit generated names and field survey experiences with a number of prospective assistants. In some cases, preparatory time in a country even allows you to establish contacts in the very communities to which you will return for the full-blown research project.

More commonly, although collaborative relationships can and often are established by mail, preparatory visits can provide an especially valuable opportunity to establish professional affiliations and secure research clearances, which are important, if not requisite, in the competition for scarce funding. When at all possible, get letters while still in-country since an "out of sight, out of mind" mentality prevails as much among foreign bureaucrats and scholars as it does at home. Like it or not, personal connections and contacts matter enormously to the conduct of official business the world over.

Often the choice of overseas institutional affiliation is very limited because of the paucity of host country research organizations, the narrowness of the research topic, or both. But where there is some latitude, different strategies can help you choose among alternative collaborators. One is to select the institution with the best reputation, either for funders or for informants to whom one might present a letter of introduction on institutional letterhead. An alternative is to affiliate with the organization that seems most likely to provide the greatest support for the proposed research project. In the best of all possible worlds, these two strategies coincide, but often they do not.

Many researchers interviewed for this book were able to get logistical support (e.g., an office; a computer; a vehicle; access to phone, fax, photocopier, library, or lab), valuable assistance in negotiating bureaucratic obstacles, or academic guidance from host country sponsors. Most important, such an active affiliation can mean that research does not take place in a vacuum; it has palpable links to host country academic and policy-making circles. A host country affiliation can thus be a boon to the overseas fieldworker. One researcher rightly reminded us to "consider exactly what you as a researcher can give to your collaborators on a daily basis, since you are likely to take quite a bit from them in the course of your visit."

Still, many prospective host country sponsors are understandably wary of foreigners looking for an institutional or organizational affiliation. Too often, skills, data, and information flow in one direction, and host country scholars often tire of such parasitic experiences. So, too, do their years of exposure to pontificating foreign "experts" sometimes yield impatience with visiting researchers. Some sponsors are suspicious of the motives of visiting researchers and project onto them commercial ambition, partisan political agendas, or intelligence-gathering functions, regardless of whether such motives exist. Moreover, more than one host country scholar has had brilliant research ideas pirated, without acknowledgment, by foreign visitors with the advantage of superior access to the necessary research funds. In some places such experiences (and opportunism) have prompted local institutions to demand substantial fees or a share of one's research grant money in exchange for the privilege of affiliation. Under such circumstances the costs of affiliation might exceed the benefits, so you should clearly establish the requirements for affiliation before committing to a professional relationship.

The shorter the period spent in-country on a preliminary site visit, the more important it is to inform people in advance of the impending longer visit and, where possible, to prearrange meetings. In general, talk to as many people as possible in the time available. One researcher reported having built up the list of useful people with whom to meet by getting the names of two or three more people from each person with whom he met. He, like several other respondents, gave a one-page summary of his research project to those who were interested, and also brought along a couple of copies of his entire dissertation proposal, which was extremely useful on one important occasion. Business cards are likewise essential for making introductions in many countries.

Often it is possible to bring home secondary data and work through it carefully between field periods. Armed with secondary data and interview notes from an exploratory research trip, you can refine theoretical models and empirical methods with the aid of advisers and colleagues who may be largely unreachable from the field. If you are able to collect field questionnaires used by other researchers as well as other survey instruments, you can often prepare a first draft of your primary data collection materials (ready for pretesting) before returning to the field.

Several scholars observed that it is a good idea to undertake an exploratory research trip even if you have been to the site before. If your previous exposure has not been in a research context, prior acquaintance may engender a false sense of familiarity. Even a brief exploratory research trip allows you the opportunity to read the newspapers, listen to radio programs, and talk with people to see if the original research design properly identifies the issues and actors. Northern scholars commonly approach questions in an unfamiliar society with tools and understanding gleaned from places with which they are more familiar, but which may be inappropriate or irrelevant. This can be dangerous because placing problems in a specific context is crucial to produce analysis that is both accurate and relevant.

The preparatory visit also allows you to get a feel for living conditions at the research site. By noting what goods and services are available in satisfactory quality, quantity, and price, you can quickly identify which items to bring for the longer haul and which to leave home. You can also learn the idiosyncrasies of local telecommunications and work out appropriate contingency plans. Especially for those who leave family at home, this can save considerable expense and anxiety in the long run. Likewise, learning about the health situation and services, housing options, and host country banking services can preempt many of the crises that inevitably consume inordinate amounts of research time. Just making a few contacts and becoming familiar with the physical layout of the place, the food, and the ambiance can go a long way toward relieving the inevitable anxiety you experience in advance of departure for the "real thing." As Devereux and Hoddinott (1993, 10) noted, "One major anxiety all fieldworkers feel is the urge to get the research under way as soon after arrival as possible (to 'hit the ground running'), and the temptation to rush things is that much greater if the ground has not been cleared in advance." In one way or another, virtually all scholars we spoke with stressed that some prior acquaintance with "the field" is highly desirable, if not essential, to a successful research experience overseas.

In short, a preliminary trip allows you time to test the feasibility of the original research design and to rethink carefully the entire project before committing fully to its execution. Often the feasibility, relevance, and desirability of a year or more committed to research in a foreign location can be properly evaluated only from first-hand, practical experience. Several scholars who did not undertake a short preliminary visit desperately wished they had. At a minimum, the site(s), timing, questions, or methods of research get fine-tuned according to current conditions prevailing in the host country. Moreover, it is not uncommon for researchers to revise their projects dramatically after an exploratory visit, even to settle on sites in countries other than those initially visited or on completely different topics. This can forestall the sort of panic experienced by Will Reno and facilitate a productive transition, such as he made (see below).

Most fundamental, many (especially young) researchers carry with them to the field romantic notions about foreign societies. An exploratory research trip often serves a valuable purpose in disabusing you of distracting preconceived notions, thus permitting more careful

---

Changing the Research Topic in Midstream

One month into my research sojourn in Sierra Leone to study the politics of agricultural reform, a crisis over my research agenda was brewing. Any six-year-old small child on the street knew that "reform" in Sierra Leone was a joke. Fourah Bay College students laughed at my research plans. "What *is* the real story here?" I asked. "Corruption," was the reply. I fell into a depression. My research proposal contained only the lies I read in official documents I collected in the U.S. before my departure. Here I was, thousands of miles from home, months to go in my stay, and I [would have to] return home with no dissertation topic, quit school, and beg for quarters in front of the university library.

It hit me as I was walking along a path in the nearby forest preserve: study how the country really works. A simple proposition, to be sure, but difficult to operationalize, since most politics takes place through manipulation of black markets. So, I set out to study how political leaders use black markets to manage rivals and reward supporters, a topic that eventually netted me a book contract. The end result, however, bore virtually no resemblance to the original research proposal.

WILL RENO

study and understanding of the complex realities of the site. One young scholar reported back to the SSRC:

> Another area in which my "thinking" is still evolving as a result of my year in Central America has to do with the positional politics of being a "First World" leftist intellectual studying peripheral societies. While I have always been aware of the obvious paradox involved in studying subaltern groups and societies from the privileged vantage point of the well-supported U.S. academy, I found myself facing a more personal aspect of this problem last year. I came to realize that, on an emotional level, I did not like Costa Rican culture or Costa Rican society. . . . In short, I found myself . . . projecting onto [Costa Ricans] the qualities I disliked most about North American culture. As I came to understand this—and the contradictions of such a position—I think I gained not only a keener insight into the illusions of leftist romanticism, but also a more nuanced understanding of real popular aspirations, at least in Central America.

You cannot presume to do more than scratch the surface of a foreign culture in a visit of a few weeks or months, but becoming aware of some subtleties can help to prepare you for the field and can help in research design.

Language Training

Although it was once taken as gospel that aptitude in the local language was a prerequisite to fieldwork, empirical social scientists now dispute whether competence in the native language of a research site is necessary or even desirable, given the considerable time and money spent on language study. Devereux (1993, 44) put this best:

> Language impinges on both major components of fieldwork— the research exercise and the social or personal aspect. From both points of view, there can be little doubt that fluency is preferable to total incomprehension. . . . If acquiring fluency were an entirely costless procedure, therefore, there might be a case for insisting that this should be a prerequisite for every fieldworker.
>
> But learning the language is a "data collection exercise" in its own right, and the investment of valuable time and intellectual

energy in acquiring this knowledge should be assessed alongside the imperative to collect other types of data. Even if the benefits of fluency are sizeable, this time and energy might be better employed doing other things.

An exploratory research trip provides probably the best gauge of the level of language ability needed to execute the planned research. Moreover, language study can often be combined with other objectives (such as those described above) in an exploratory research trip.

For those who need or want to undertake intensive language study before field research, there remains the important choice of whether to study language in-country or at home, perhaps at an intensive language program such as those run in the summer at any number of colleges and universities. Most experts assert that an immersive environment is the key to learning the language well. Programs that insist on twenty-four-hour-a-day dedication to the target language—no English—win high marks from virtually all commentators.

Ironically, overseas training might not always be the best choice. Although it carries the benefit of allowing a person to live in an environment where the target language is also a living language, other problems can arise. Texts and instructors can be of low or uneven quality. Instructional methods frequently emphasize rote learning, especially in difficult languages. Unfamiliarity with the environment often induces foreigners to spend time together, so that study overseas may actually undermine the attainment of true language immersion. Moreover, unless your skills in the target language are already far better than most locals' skills in English, many conversations naturally turn to English, either because the native speakers are trying to be helpful or because they want to improve their English.

While language skills are clearly crucial for much overseas research, you may not need to be fluent. Establish up front the level of fluency needed to implement your research design successfully and the most effective means to reach that level. Moreover, establish clearly which language is necessary; the official language of a country is often inappropriate to a particular regional site. Keep in mind that insufficient language skills are one of the primary reasons projects fail, and funding agencies will be much more likely to turn down grant proposals if these skills are inadequate.

Finding Funding

Selecting a site and finding funding are often interrelated, with funding frequently depending upon the choice of a particular research site and, in some cases, a site being chosen in part to attract funds. The process of financing even a relatively meager budget is rarely easy.

"Apply early, apply often." "My advice is to 'create' your way to success, by any means imaginable, unconventional, exploratory, or otherwise." "Even if the chances seem slim, APPLY!" These are typical replies we received to questions about how researchers found funding for their projects. The point is clear: Make time for fundraising. You make your own breaks in the scramble for research funding.

Leave no stone unturned. Remember that the apparent raison d'être of a multitude of organizations is to write checks to eager and capable researchers. The tedious task of ploughing through the huge grants registers is inevitable. Send simple, enthusiastic letters to any prospective sponsor that seems even remotely interested in the research topic. Do *not* send form letters, but instead study the criteria of each agency in order to understand and respond to stated interests and objectives. This does indeed take a great deal of time, but it is a necessary investment if you wish to finance a thorough research project. Such written inquiries generally elicit prompt replies indicating whether funds are available and, if they are, application deadlines and instructions. In rare but delightful cases, donors impressed with your proposed research send a small, unconditional grant simply from such letters. These small sums might not fund an entire project but can be marketed to donors offering bigger grants as a sign of others' confidence in the value of the research project. Moreover, smaller grants can provide valuable discretionary funding (to hire assistants, rent a vehicle, or buy useful equipment such as a laptop computer) in the event a more substantial award comes through.

We note that the process seems somewhat more difficult and the range of grants for which you are eligible somewhat narrower in the case of nonresident aliens (some grants are exclusively for citizens of the granting country) or those undertaking insider research. Contrary to myth, few substantial research grants (as opposed to student fellowships) are available only to minorities, much less only to those from disadvantaged areas of the world.

Overall, the process of identifying prospective sources of research funding and applying for grants generally takes months and must be initiated a year or more before you intend to leave for the field. Funding agencies then typically take several months to review applications and announce funding decisions, sometimes not leaving researchers with much time before departing for the field, even though the process may have started twelve to eighteen months earlier.

Just writing and revising a good proposal can take weeks, even months. The process involves considerable consultation with others and much rewriting. Academic experts at your home institution, leading scholars on the country or topic of interest, and especially host country researchers often provide invaluable feedback on draft proposals. Many scholars also echoed the remarks of one researcher's advocacy of exploratory field visits as a superior way to "meet with as many people as possible relevant to or interested in [your] research in order to garner more insight and suggestions to improve [your] proposal." Diligence and a thick skin are the keys to accepting and profiting from the inevitable and not-always-constructive criticism. That said, there are exceptional cases in which clearly important research topics undertaken by unusually skilled researchers get funded despite an extremely brief proposal-writing period. One researcher, who won a Fulbright grant despite dashing off the application the day after returning from an exploratory trip to the research site, attributes her success to the enthusiasm palpable in her proposal.

The preparation of successful grant proposals is an art in itself. There is no simple recipe to ensure success in the sometimes brutal competition for research funding. Nonetheless, several consistent themes emerge from the scholars we consulted. First, the proposal must offer a clear and concise statement of the question you seek to answer and a strong argument as to why it is important to answer that question. Recognizing that busy people from assorted disciplines read scores of grant applications in the screening process, you should write your proposal in simple, declarative sentences. Attempting to demonstrate the complexity of a problem in a grant proposal is likely to prove counterproductive. When possible, directly connect everything that follows the initial thesis statement—theoretical arguments, literature review, discussions of research design and methodology, your qualifications to complete the proposed research—back to the main argument. It sounds simple but is, in fact, very difficult for unpracticed researchers. It is often helpful to look at other proposals, both successful and unsuccessful, as a guide.

Second, identify the interests and objectives of the funding agency, and tailor the proposal accordingly. Most good scholarly research shows promise on more than one level, including theoretical advances, methodological innovations, and contributions to current political debates. Thus, you can emphasize one or another dimension to different prospective donors without misrepresenting yourself. Moreover, this teasing out of different threads in the overall research project is not only useful for winning a grant, but often contributes considerably to the quality of the final research product.

Third, one of the most valuable items in a successful grant application for overseas research is a letter of invitation from a host institution, indicating an interest in the proposed research and a willingness to facilitate the project. As mentioned earlier, exploratory visits are a common means by which to secure strong letters from host country institutions and scholars. Unless specifically prohibited, feel free to amend a grant application with supplementary materials, especially letters of recommendation from host country institutions and scholars or research clearances already obtained.

Fourth, be realistic about research design. The broader and more ambitious the project, the more wary funding agencies become about its feasibility. For example, visiting multiple countries increases the risk that you will encounter serious impediments to a successful research program. You might, for example, run into problems in obtaining all necessary research clearances. Given the difficulties of "settling in" (discussed in Chapter 4), funding agencies might also be concerned about the quality of the fieldwork from a project with multiple and widespread sites. Anyone who has ever fielded a survey appreciates the enormous administrative and logistical challenge of careful data collection across vast spaces and the realities of respondent fatigue. Proposed data collection must not be unrealistically broad in either scope or space.

Fifth, give careful consideration to those asked to write recommendations on behalf of the proposed research and researcher. Not all recommenders carry equal weight with grantsmaking institutions, nor does the relative value of your adviser's words of praise remain constant across donors. But a blind preference for the most prominent scholars carries with it obvious dangers. You need recommenders who can credibly convey an intimate knowledge of the proposed research and abundant confidence in your abilities to complete the project successfully. A mix of references who are familiar with the project and researcher and those who are well known worked well for many contributors who won major research grants.

It is difficult to advise on the optimal level of specificity in grant proposals. Most people provide reasonably precise identification of a site and timing. Nevertheless, all funding agencies understand that sites and schedules sometimes change (although they might not support dramatic changes). The more ideal your site for the proposed research, the more sense it makes to trumpet this advantage. Just recognize that unforeseen circumstances, such as civil unrest or denial of research clearance, may force you to change sites. If the strength of the grant proposal rests entirely on a single site, which becomes infeasible, the funding agency might not approve a revised research design. Thus some researchers insert "mobility clauses" into grant applications, and most avoid pinning everything on one precisely defined locale.

Most prospective donors require a research project budget. Inexperienced respondents routinely cite budgeting as a confusing, frustrating exercise in naive forecasting. For most researchers undertaking their first study in a country, budgeting is a process of gathering scraps of information and making intelligent guesses. The best way to gather the necessary information is through personal observation during an exploratory visit. You might also want to rely on contacts who have done recent research in the site or country, advisers with fieldwork experience, and natives of the research site.

Most dissertators underestimate the budgetary requirements of their research projects. Some deliberately underestimate the budget, assuming that asking for "too much" might jeopardize the chances of receiving a grant, although there is little factual basis to support this. Moreover, researchers funded on an unnecessarily skimpy budget often live to regret having too little to properly fund data collection, analysis, and basic survival. A special problem often arises for researchers going to economies experiencing high inflation: currency devaluation can throw even a well-researched budget completely out of whack. Those heading to such places need to be especially careful not to underestimate the financial requirements of the project, for funding agencies do not always adjust award levels to account for even severe macroeconomic shocks. Keep in mind as well that changes in exchange rates—which can be dramatic in either direction—can also have an enormous impact on how much money you need.

In budgeting, break down expenses by category (international travel, in-country travel, supplies, assistants' compensation, etc.). Do not presume that shortfalls will cancel out across categories. Some donors provide unconditional financing, but other grants' fungibility is sharply limited. For instance, some prohibit surplusses in international travel from being transferred to cover shortfalls in the budget for materials and supplies. Where no set form is provided, many who are expert in grant writing recommend identifying not just the uses of funds but also the sources. Indicate funding already secured, including any personal savings or borrowing committed to the project. Others' willingness to put money behind the project helps defuse concerns about the value and viability of the proposed research. Whether they expressly acknowledge it or not, most grantsmakers like cofinancing.

Researchers who have done their homework, have an interesting subject and appropriate method, and are very lucky sometimes win multiple grants. It is imperative that you report the full range of grants awarded to each granting agency so as to avoid overlapping funding. At the margin this often permits funding one of an agency's alternate grantees. Even with overlapping contributions eliminated, multiple grants generally yield more generous funding because different agencies pay for different sorts of expenses. Thus one of the coauthors was able to combine four grants to pay for the considerable expenses involved in fielding a large, formal survey and subsequent analysis.

Moreover, it is often true that money begets money. Receiving a fellowship that pays for a preparatory visit to your research site—or that frees you from other (teaching or research) obligations—often provides the additional insights and time necessary to acquire more substantial funding. Prior funding can also establish you as a "good risk," thereby improving your prospects for receiving funding. So begin the process early.

One scholar, herself a recipient of both Fulbright and SSRC dissertation funding, summed up succinctly: "I do not believe that there is any way to 'finesse' the application process. One must simply have a strong, well written and well argued proposal, submit all of the information that they are looking for, and get the application in neatly and on time."

What to do if you do not get (enough) funding? First, and above all, you must not lose confidence. The number of qualified applicants in most grant competitions far exceeds the limit of grantsmakers' funds.

Sometimes award decisions can appear arbitrary, responding to fashions or the historical prejudices of a particular agency (or, more precisely, its external reviewers) due to an inability to distinguish among equally meritorious proposals. Every experienced field researcher has been turned down, often frequently.

That said, if funding is not forthcoming for one approach to the project, rethink the proposal, and perhaps reorient it slightly to hook into a larger, preexisting project. Write letters to other scholars working in the field, but expect no response; they owe you nothing. Nonetheless, you may be pleasantly surprised at the fruitful advice and opportunities that result from such attempts.

Consider alternative methods of funding your research. Some researchers fund fieldwork (or the extension of a research project begun on a grant) through a professional services contract with a development or conservation agency or with a business. Consulting opportunities abound for researchers in-country with decent academic credentials and good skills and contacts. The crucial consideration regarding such arrangements is whether efforts undertaken under terms of the contract support the original research program sufficiently without compromising academic integrity.

Loans are generally available, either explicitly through a financial institution, friend, or relative, or implicitly through credit card use. But loans can be dangerous if they tempt you to skimp on necessary research expenses. Also, if debt servicing induces excessive moonlighting or premature acceptance of permanent employment, borrowing may ultimately degrade the quality of your work. On the other hand, concerns about finishing up before you need to start repaying a debt can also fuel uncommon industriousness, at least according to one scholar who resorted to this method. When absolutely necessary, borrowing appears best left to the writeup stage of a research project, where the risks of cutting corners in data collection are lowest and the need to motivate analysis is sometimes highest.

Finally, you can always search for a preexisting research project on your chosen topic or in your preferred site. It can be tough to crack the lineup of an established effort, but such opportunities do arise. One good way to start such a search is to contact the operations officers at large donor organizations (e.g., USAID, World Bank) to find out which institutions or individuals have large contracts in force in your area of interest.

Summary

The early stages of defining and funding an overseas research project take a great deal of time and energy. Although most of us hunger to get on with the "real research" and to finish with the annoying administrative, logistical, and emotional preliminaries, researchers consistently advise taking your time in these initial stages. If you rush through site selection and the search for sufficient funding, it will come back to haunt you. Perhaps the most useful advice from the scholars we consulted is not to become impatient or dismayed by delays, changes of plans, or rejections. Consider them not just the price of progress but also practice for the field. Patience and perseverance are crucial all along the way, both at home and in the field.

3

Predeparture Preparations

Once decided on the site and with funding secured, you still have countless things to worry about before leaving home. In this chapter we suggest some of the issues you need to consider before heading overseas, including many things you might not imagine necessary at first glance. The list ranges from the obvious to the obscure, and we suggest different strategies for approaching the inevitable obstacles of life overseas. We focus on both life's essentials (health, money, family, housing) and academic essentials (contacts, research clearance). Not everything can be done before departure, but there is truth to the adage that "preparation prevents poor performance."

We offer one blanket recommendation: Consult with anyone you possibly can who has recently been to the site in which you will be doing research. They can advise on where you might live, whom you might contact, and other site-specific information. For general information on local conditions, contact the Council on International Educational Exchange (which administers Fulbright grants); it provides recent reports on living and research conditions in many countries.

Money and Travel

Practically speaking, issues of money are primary. If you mishandle money, the entire research trip can be disastrous. Much depends on the state of financial technology in the host country. In some countries, you can depend on an ATM card issued by a bank based in the United States (or linked to a network that allows withdrawal of funds from a U.S. bank account). In other countries you must carry cash.

Put your financial affairs in order before leaving. Bills will have to be paid while you are gone. Most researchers ensure that such obligations are covered by giving a relative or a trustworthy friend formal power of attorney before leaving. Although many rely on family or friends to handle financial matters, some scholars find it more practical to use a U.S. bank's billpayer services, through which you can pay a fee to the bank and have the bank pay the bills while you are away. Regardless of whether or not you use such a service, bank contacts can be helpful, especially if problems arise later. Finally, consultation with a lawyer may be necessary for more complex matters than paying bills.

Keep in mind that initial costs can be substantial, especially if you are going to be abroad for an extended period of time. Expect to incur some debt at the outset of the project if your personal resources are limited. Some researchers rely on loans from parents or relatives, while others take on student loans or more expensive debt, such as credit cards. Whatever the financing, it is often necessary to plan to spend more money initially than a grant's first payment(s) provide. Most researchers will agree that going into limited initial debt is worthwhile when launching a research project.

Get and carry a credit card that offers field services, not just financing. Some cards grant holders access to mail services while abroad, or permit you to write checks on a home bank account to receive traveler's checks. Fast and reliable international replacement of a lost or stolen credit card is necessary. The utility of such a service clearly depends on your access to the card issuer's offices. These tend to be confined to cities, so researchers in remote areas might find a credit card of little use. One researcher illustrated the benefits of an American Express card as follows: "I was robbed on a bus in Buenos Aires. I was getting off the bus when I felt a push. After I got off the bus I realized that my wallet was gone. I immediately went home to cancel my credit cards. After phoning about half a dozen telephone numbers, I was finally able to report the theft of my card. The operator told me to report to the Amex office on the next day, and my new Gold Card would be waiting." Other credit card companies offer similar services, and it is wise to check before leaving home.

Credit cards are not always advisable, of course, especially when doing research in rural areas or in countries with a high inflation rate.

One of the coauthors encountered a striking reluctance on the part of merchants to accept credit cards (and found that the use of credit cards greatly increased prices) when inflation rates were high, since merchants received payments from banks for the incurred charges well after the purchase was made, reducing the real value of their sale. Nevertheless, when they can be used, credit cards often provide a superior (interbank) exchange rate, depending on the local currency regulations. Investigate such regulations before going to the field.

Traveler's checks are another option, sometimes more convenient than credit cards since virtually any foreign exchange office accepts traveler's checks. That said, foreign exchange offices are often confined to banks and airports. So, like credit cards, traveler's checks may not work well outside of major urban centers since formal financial networks are often thin or missing in the hinterland. Carrying cash is always a risky option, but a necessary one in some places. When carrying cash, investigate whether exchanging large or small bills is easier. Look into the possibility of setting up a bank account in the host country. Its practicality will depend on local banking regulations, but access to a local account can alleviate the need to carry cash or traveler's checks and minimize the time it takes to deal with the local financial system.

In deciding how to get to the research site, shop around for good airfares. Major U.S. newspapers carry advertisements for ticket brokers that can save hundreds of dollars in travel expenses. Research and patience are especially important if your family accompanies you abroad, since grants seldom cover dependents' travel. That said, one researcher pointed out that low-cost student tickets are usually quite inflexible, a problem if you need to change flight schedules due to an emergency, delayed research clearance, or other problems. It is also advisable to invest in travel insurance for luggage and research materials. Once you relinquish your apartment or house in the United States, renter's insurance generally no longer covers your possessions.

Health

There is nothing worse than being caught unprepared for an illness or an emergency. Although you cannot anticipate everything, some general guidelines can help in planning for a relatively healthy time abroad and, should things go wrong, for emergencies.

First, establish what immunization shots you need before going to the field. Your home health provider should be able to identify necessary immunizations for any given site at any given time. The U.S. Centers for Disease Control in Atlanta update this information as needed and can fax or electronically mail requested information on specific countries or parts of the world (phone: 404/332-4555; fax: 404/332-4565). Another useful source for advice is the International Association for Medical Assistance to Travelers (417 Center St., Lewiston, NY 14092), which provides up-to-date information on good hospitals in foreign countries, disease prevalence, and inoculations. It is also a good idea to contact host country health officials (e.g., at the nearest consulate or embassy) to find out which immunizations are needed for entry. Begin this process earlier rather than later, since some immunizations (e.g., hepatitis B or plague vaccinations) require a sequence of shots spaced out over several months. It is also worth consulting health specialists familiar with the research site regarding the best way to sterilize food and water. In many places, for instance, it is necessary to soak vegetables and fruits in chlorinated water before cooking and eating them. In some places filtration systems work well, while in others chemical sterilization is more effective. Boiling water, while almost always the best way to sterilize water, takes a lot of time and cooking fuel, both of which may be scarce.

More generally, it is highly desirable to be in good physical and mental shape prior to departure. A new environment and diet, exposure to foreign vectors, and the stress of launching a major research initiative can take a toll on your health, especially on an immune system weakened by inactivity, stress, or fatigue.

All this said, most field researchers fall ill no matter how well they prepare themselves. So plan accordingly, taking a good first-aid kit, including syringes if the sterility of the blood supply and medical equipment is questionable. You might also want to consider purchasing a copy of David Werner's *Where There Is No Doctor*. As the name suggests, this book can come in handy in emergencies, but it is also a good reference for more common ailments. One scholar offered the following sensible advice:

> My policy is to play it safe, and I have never had more than a slight stomach upset while doing fieldwork in Africa. Even after living in Africa over fifteen years, I do not eat "street food," no matter how good it smells and regardless of how much I want to identify with the informal sector. I am careful about eating un-

cooked vegetables in restaurants. I drink soda or tea when I am not sure whether the water was boiled. I use a mosquito net . . . and I am not a hypochondriac!

You also need to think about health insurance. If your grant includes it, make sure that the provided insurance covers all your needs. It is much less likely that a spouse's health insurance (much less an unmarried partner's) will be provided; thus, you may need to purchase supplemental insurance. Insurance can be expensive, so financial planning (and grant budgeting) should take such costs into account. Grants-making organizations and international programs offices at major universities can usually recommend insurance providers, but it pays to compare plans. Furthermore, one researcher made a point of recommending that you should know in advance *exactly* how to file a claim.

In addition to general health insurance, consider the possibility of potential disasters. This is particularly important for those who will be some distance away from high quality medical care and therefore might need rapid medical evacuation. Under such circumstances, think seriously about purchasing evacuation insurance, such as that provided by SOS of Philadelphia. Furthermore (without meaning to sound alarmist), one researcher who worked in Africa noted that "one or one's family might want to take out a life insurance policy on the researcher (my mother did!!!). Sounds very grim—but there are considerable expenses involved in bringing a body back from overseas and if [such funds] might not be readily or easily available, then a life insurance policy payment might help." Medical evacuation insurance policies often contain a repatriation rider to cover this contingency. Embassies (individually or as a multinational co-op) often maintain a blood bank in areas where the sterility of hospitals and the screening of the local blood supply are poor. It is thus worth checking whether you can participate in such a plan, as insurance and for peace of mind in the event of an accident or emergency surgery.

You can prepare for common illnesses. First, establish which diseases are endemic to the region and season of your research. If malaria is widespread, find out whether local strains are chloroquine resistant and know the recommended preventative measures. When working in a malarial area, take along a mosquito net, especially the tent type, which fully seals a sleeping area. Insect repellent or smoke coils often help keep mosquitoes away. Finally, given the AIDS epidemic world-wide, proper protection and precautions regarding transmission of the HIV virus and other sexually transmitted diseases are absolutely essential.

Intestinal problems are common for many overseas researchers, often due to parasites. One researcher warned that "the worst thing you can do in that case is take an over-the-counter diarrhea medicine like Pepto Bismol or Maalox. These medicines act like corks, and they just stop you up, allowing the parasite to go on living and reproducing thousands of times in your system." Depending on the nature of the illness, an antibiotic may be necessary, though be wary of self-diagnosis. As one scholar advised, "If the illness is serious enough to consider taking something, then it [is] serious enough to consult a doctor. . . . Regardless of the state of local medical facilities, local doctors are likely to know more about illnesses in the area than someone who has only recently arrived."

Another set of problems confronts those with preexisting medical conditions who may need to bring large amounts of prescription medications. In regions where drug traffic is common, you may be asked to open bottles or show a prescription. So be prepared with a letter from your doctor stating your condition and special needs. This can help with both government and medical authorities.

Keep in mind that if you are going to hire research assistants, it is your responsibility to provide for their health care as well. As one economist who utilized several research assistants put it, "I don't think anyone on the project should feel less well protected than another." Given the privileged position in which most northern researchers find themselves, this seems a sound principle.

Having your children with you in the field presents special health concerns, since they tend to be more susceptible to illnesses and need more frequent preventive and curative care. The above recommendations also apply to children, although you need to pay special attention to vaccinations and malaria prophylaxis, some of which are too powerful for small children. Consult with a pediatrician well in advance of taking young children overseas. As most researchers who have gone abroad with children will attest, responsibility for children generally heightens parents' sensitivity to health-related issues. Ironically, oftentimes, the care given to children's health is not always extended to oneself. One researcher commented that he and his wife "would have been well-advised to consistently follow the same precautions" they did for their child. When accompanied to the field by children, consult with your pediatrician about any special precautions that should be taken. Identify a pediatrician as soon as you arrive on site, if not before. One researcher noted that an effective way to find a pediatrician is to consult with local day care providers. Local academic contacts and recommendations from the expatriate community also often prove helpful. Take your children's medical records with you, including the yellow vaccination booklet.

We also recommend that if you take your child with you, get a notarized letter from each parent authorizing that either parent may travel alone with the child if necessary and that the child be able to travel alone in case of emergency. Getting a child her own passport and visas is wise, and often required.

Housing

The key to finding satisfactory housing is simple to articulate but difficult to execute: You have to be happy where you are living. There is nothing worse than coming home from a difficult day of dealing with bureaucrats or interviewing farmers to a place that you find uncomfortable or depressing. The trick is to find a place you deem acceptable financially and psychologically.

Looking for housing takes a lot of time, either before going to the field, upon arriving, or both. We discuss the search for a dwelling after your arrival on site in the next chapter; here we focus briefly on what you can do before leaving.

Ideally, you should settle housing arrangements before leaving. Usually, this proves impossible; most researchers find a place to live after they arrive. Those who reported success in lining up housing prior to arrival were able to do so because of local contacts established earlier. Most such contacts were made on previous research trips. It is obviously much easier to set up housing before arrival if you are familiar with the layout of the city or village.

More frequently, however, the most you can do from home is to arrange for temporary housing. This is probably safer, in any event, if you have not seen the apartment or house on offer. The expatriate community often has embassy guest houses or knows of a family on extended vacation that would welcome a housesitter, so early contact with embassy contacts can be fruitful. You might also be able to arrange to stay with friends at the research site, which can serve as a base from which to look for more permanent lodging. One researcher also suggested church guest houses. These arrangements can provide a homey atmosphere and useful contacts. In any of these arrangements, you should be careful about overstaying your welcome.

The most common short-term lodging preparation is to reserve a hotel room for your date of arrival. If the hotel arrangements are unsatisfactory, you can always change hotels. One researcher's experience shows several sides of the option:

> In a desperate move to have some illusion of security and "home" in the field, I reserved an apartment in a hotel in the downtown area before I left. . . . This turned out to be financially costly, psychically isolating, and damaging to my reputation. Being a woman staying in a hotel notorious for being a place where expatriates find Kenyan lovers did not help my attempts to be professional and above reproach. Nonetheless, reserving the hotel room did give me some peace of mind for the period during which I was preparing to leave the States and traveling to Kenya . . . and gave me a base from which to locate alternative housing, which I eventually did.

In the next chapter we will discuss in more detail some of the important issues involved in looking for a more permanent abode.

Packing: What to Bring, What to Leave

Most researchers report that they mispacked when they went to the field, either bringing unnecessary items or forgetting absolutely essential (though easily overlooked) ones. There are no general rules here, and much depends on where and when you are going, and your personal preferences. Again, an exploratory research visit can clarify the issue. In this section we simply list what researchers have reported as "essentials" they forgot and "nonessentials" that weighed down their bags and took up space. Not all will be relevant to everyone, but the listing should provide a starting point. Research equipment and ancillary tools are addressed separately in Chapter 5.

Do not forget:

✈ BUSINESS CARDS. In urban areas in particular, business cards can prove essential. Information on it should include: name, address, phone, fax, e-mail, and telex, if available, as well as your affiliation and title. Introduce yourself with a card and expect to receive one in return. It is a serious professional *faux pas* in many cultures not to have a card. For whatever reason, having cards adds an air of seriousness to your endeavor. If you can get them embossed with your home institution's seal, all the better. The more that one is dealing with elites in one's research, the more necessary are business cards.

✦ TOILETRIES. What is needed obviously depends on what is available in-country. You will want to consult with those who have been to the research site recently. What you bring will also depend on what you consider "essential," and how much change of routine you can handle without getting frustrated. Recognize that even in countries where the same brands as at home can be found, they are often much more expensive overseas, sometimes by a factor of two or three. For this reason, some experienced researchers recommend bringing a reasonable supply of the following items: shampoo, hair conditioner, sunscreen, insect repellent, tampons, vitamin supplements, towelettes or moist hand wipes, contact lens paraphernalia, and skin moisturizer.

✦ EXTRA EYEGLASSES OR CONTACT LENSES. These are often difficult or expensive to replace, so take at least one extra pair.

✦ TRAVEL IRON. This can prove invaluable if you expect to travel a lot and need to maintain a respectable appearance.

✦ BIRTH CONTROL. Many researchers report that finding any manner of birth control is difficult. Some also report that even where they are available, the quality of condoms sold in some countries is questionable. Enough said.

✦ A LOCAL LANGUAGE/ENGLISH DICTIONARY. This is something most researchers find essential, unless they are truly fluent in the language of the host country.

✦ AN INTERNATIONAL STUDENT IDENTITY CARD. Depending on location, an ISIC comes in handy when purchasing discounted air tickets, obtaining reduced admission to museums, etc.

✦ A FLASHLIGHT. Especially crucial in areas subject to frequent blackouts, or in places where access to electricity is limited. Do not forget a spare bulb; these can be excruciatingly difficult to find overseas.

✦ PEPPER SPRAY. One researcher noted that "it is a good item for any woman to carry. I always had mine in my bag and there were a couple of times that I almost had to use it and was relieved that it was there."

✈ ELECTRICAL ADAPTERS. Find out the kind of outlet(s) the country uses, as well as the voltage typically available (it may be different in rural and urban areas of the same country) to see if an adapter is necessary.

✈ RECHARGEABLE BATTERIES AND BATTERY CHARGER. These can come in handy and, in addition to being ecologically sensible, can save a substantial amount of money when using a tape recorder in interviews or a tape player for music.

✈ CHILDREN'S POSSESSIONS. One researcher reported that, "especially with small kids, it was absolutely necessary to take along . . . toys, blankets, books, etc. . . . Nothing fouls up great research plans quicker than distraught kids, and the dislocation of a new house, new school, no friends and a strange place can be quite unsettling to kids of a certain age. We took along more than I thought was necessary at the time, but it turned out to be the bare minimum. It is worth excess baggage [charges] to soften the impact of displacement on young kids." In a related vein, another researcher noted that one of the best things that he and his wife brought along to the field was a book on child development and health care, which gave them great peace of mind.

✈ AUTOMATIC-DRIP COFFEEPOT. For those of us who need a jolt of caffeine to get started in the morning, this little luxury can be a lifesaver. One researcher said she "smiled at it every morning."

✈ SHORTWAVE RADIO. Where the local press is heavily censored or in remote areas, a shortwave radio can be a valuable link to the outside world. It can also be a useful research tool for tracking the local reporting of domestic and international events.

✈ OFFICE SUPPLIES. Bring from home such things as academic department letterhead, containers for mailing diskettes, and Post-It notes, which can be hard to come by (or are very expensive) in the research site.

✈ PLEASURE READING. A few novels or other books completely unconnected to one's own work will be a welcome diversion from research, from which distraction is often necessary.

✈ A FIRST-AID KIT. There will be ample opportunity to use it, for others as well for as yourself. Keep it small and lightweight, though it is well worth the baggage space.

Lest you feel we are adding only to the burden of packing, experienced scholars consistently offered the following two recommendations on what could safely be left at home, usually without serious consequences.

✈ ACADEMIC BOOKS AND OTHER ACADEMIC MATERIALS. Many researchers lamented having brought so much of their "essential" work materials with them. Academic books and files of articles are, of course, nice to have for handy reference (and taking a *few* is sensible). There will be times when you wish you had your entire file cabinet along, but the truth of it is, most of your time will be spent exploring and tracking new information. Certainly, while in the field, you will be attempting to fit this new information into frameworks, ideas, and theories contained in your personal library, but it is rarely necessary to have these physically at hand. As one researcher noted,

I did send along about twenty-five books in advance of my arrival. My adviser tried to dissuade me [from] this, and ultimately I believe that he was right. These were core books in my field that I thought I would have time to read or that I might need in the event of having to make a presentation, etc. I may have read a few but never used any for a presentation. I would strongly advise against bringing any or many books into the field; they only become a nuisance as one moves around and even more so when it comes time to leave the field. They will almost certainly not be read or used. One will have all one can do to read the new material gathered in the field.

Since there will almost certainly be plenty of heavy materials in the form of newly acquired books, photocopies, other field data, and surveys to bring back, you probably do not want to add to the burden.

✈ CLOTHING. Many researchers pack an unmanageably large wardrobe for fieldwork. In particular, articles requiring special care (e.g., dry cleaning) often prove expensive to maintain and are worn infrequently. Clothes take a beating in rudimentary laundering and in the wear and tear of rugged areas, so do not take articles you cannot bear to see ripped, faded, or otherwise damaged. Moreover, you can purchase clothing overseas. Although sometimes of mediocre quality, the clothing available locally is often better suited to the climate than that available at home. Nevertheless, a caveat is in order: you need to pay attention to appearance, and we (and a number of our contributors) suggest you make a serious effort to adapt to local sensibilities, which may include jacket and tie for men and skirts or dresses for women, as Aili Tripp points out opposite.

Family Matters

For those with families (broadly defined), a crucial decision concerns whether to take them to the field. In an ideal world, one would almost always want to take loved ones along, but in reality many obstacles stand in the way. Considerations in making the decision include, among other things, a spouse/partner's career and potential work opportunities at home and abroad, the length of time away from home, the intensity of the research work, the amount of travel to expect while in the field, the potential threats to the family's health and safety, and the additional expense of having the family with you. If there are children, there is also the matter of schooling or day care. The adjustment costs (including time) of settling a family generally preclude bringing them along on short research trips. But the emotional toll of extended separation makes it difficult to leave them home for longer durations.

Choosing to leave the family at home almost inevitably increases the stress felt by both the researcher and the family. All miss the daily companionship unique to a long-term relationship or the joys and frustrations of parenthood. The research experience is, after all, an intense one, and most researchers want to share this experience with companions. The inability to do so can be frustrating, even debilitating. One researcher who was away for six months during one stretch and ten in another found it too taxing alone: "I, like most people who decide to do international research, am an independent kind of person. This does not mean, though, that living alone in a foreign country is easy [for me] . . . I don't think I want to live alone overseas for this length of time again." Indeed, long stretches without a partner can be especially taxing. Visits from the family may need to be planned. When family does visit, another researcher advised taking "some time off work. . . . It might be interesting for them to see you at work for awhile, but, especially if they don't speak the local language, they might eventually feel neglected."

If the family stays behind, make appropriate arrangements for them before leaving, especially if there are children. With children at home, a support group for the remaining spouse is absolutely essential. The absence of one parent seriously upsets family life, and everything pos-

Dressing the Part in the Field

Depending on the topic and the person being interviewed, it may be necessary to maintain a more "professional" appearance than what is acceptable or desirable among grad students studying in the United States. One need not go broke or have an extensive wardrobe, but in many cultures an excessively casual appearance (e.g., jeans, T-shirts, cutoffs) may have some negative consequences for one's research. Dressing in an overly casual manner may imply that you do not respect yourself or that you do not respect the people with whom you are coming into contact. It may also suggest that you are not dressing according to your status and therefore are showing disrespect [to the interviewee], and it may reveal a certain amount of immaturity. In addition, it may give the impression that you are younger than you are. Where we may think that dressing nicely may be a sign of being pretentious and a way of accentuating class differences, others in the country of study, even in rural areas, may think that by not dressing "properly," especially when we can afford to, we are showing a certain amount of disrespect and carelessness. For women in countries with large Muslim populations and in most African countries, shorts, long pants, and short skirts are considered clothes of prostitutes and loose women. Often people excuse it in a foreigner because they chalk it up to ignorance, but it still indicates a lack of awareness of the values of the culture one is working in.

AILI TRIPP

sible should be done to alleviate the substantial burden on the parent remaining home. Arranging extraordinary day care, helpful visitors, or even a cleaning service can help to compensate. In addition, you need to clearly agree upon ways of making contact in emergencies. Regular contact can be managed in a number of economical ways, including the use of regular mail and fax. The ever-expanding use of electronic mail certainly can make it much easier to maintain connections between home and the field, especially when telephone contact is extremely expensive (more on electronic communications in the section on academic preparations below).

There are, of course, plenty of good reasons to take your family to the field (and if they do travel with you, be sure to bring along birth and marriage certificates). As one researcher put it, "My partner and I talked about separating for a year, but I'm glad we didn't. It would have been difficult, I think, to recount the experience that I'd had. Having a partner along not only helps to pass the time, but can be an additional source of information, learning, and experience." On the other hand, the experience can also create problems for the partner. A nearly universal concern is what the partner does with her or his time during the research period. Especially if the partner is used to working or studying outside the home, it is important to put some thought into this. Finding a new routine is often especially difficult for a partner. Having children may alleviate some problems, in that it provides one with extra social opportunities, but as Darren Hawkins's comments make clear (see opposite), having children along can cut both ways.

"Nontraditional" family circumstances place special burdens on the researcher, in particular for the lesbian or gay field researcher. As one researcher explained: "Family commitments are never discussed in formal academic settings in choosing the field site. Nonetheless, families exist, often silently for the lesbian or gay researcher. . . . My experience and that of other student researchers I have observed indicate field research (as well as graduate school) favors the young, the straight, and the economically advantaged." This scholar went on to recommend some steps that the lesbian or gay researcher might take to ease the transition to field work:

> First, investigate and consider thoroughly the homophobia of
> the community to which you will relocate. . . . There may be a
> city or, more likely, a sector of a city reasonably close to your
> field site that is more tolerant of queers or is known for its
> queer community. Exploratory research will be mandatory. Take
> your partner along. If things don't turn out well, you can always
> cut it short. It's much easier to regroup from a bad exploratory
> research experience than to find out your site is unworkable
> during a more extensive period in the field. This is a worst case
> scenario, however. One can imagine many ways to accommo-
> date both a partner and safety. The arrangements will depend, in

part, on the particular field site, the local customs and cultural values toward lesbians and gays, men living together or being seen together often, which can be very different than the attitudes toward women living together or being seen together often.

Obstacles to Family Adjustment in the Field

For my wife and child, adjusting to the new culture and language was the most difficult problem we experienced and never successfully resolved. My wife had enjoyed "staying home" and being a mother in the States, but it didn't work out in Santiago [Chile]. Putting our daughter in child care wasn't really an option as she had severe stranger anxiety at the time and my wife wanted to care for her. The problem was that there was not much to do. In the States, my wife could get in the car and go to the children's museum and library, or just run errands. She could also go to [children's] play groups, La Leche League meetings, etc. Few, if any, of these options were available in Santiago. Many mothers did indeed stay at home, but seemed far more interested in cleaning their homes and cooking lunch or dinner . . . than [in] getting together [with other mothers] for anything resembling a play group. My wife spoke little Spanish and found it difficult to make friends. The lack of a car made it difficult to get around. Though the bus system is "good," it's difficult to hop on a bus that only comes to a semi-stop with a two-year-old. We did meet some North Americans with kids, but found them to be so wrapped up in their own children's schooling and so well taken care of by the U.S. embassy or multinational corporations that they had little time or interest in us. It was hard for my wife to relate to people who complained about their maids while we were struggling financially and she was experiencing high levels of culture shock. We hired a tutor, which worked out fairly nicely, except that it was also expensive. We made friends with a few neighbors, which did work out very well. But it was a daily struggle for my wife not to be bored silly.

DARREN HAWKINS

This reinforces the advice in Chapter 2: Make an exploratory research trip if at all possible.

Finally, if you take your family to a place where gender roles and customs are drastically different from those to which you are accustomed, your family must be prepared. One male researcher who had his family with him for two months in a Muslim society noted that

> very little English is spoken in Yemen, so my family was very dependent on me. Strict separation of the genders in Yemen also created difficulties for my wife; she could be with women but there was no translation. This made life difficult for her and I spent a lot of time entertaining the family. Fortunately their visit coincided with the month of Ramadan, when very little work could have been done in any case. On the other hand, the presence of my family facilitated my integration into the local community of my research site. The lone male (especially a foreigner) is perceived as socially dangerous, and the presence of my family seemed to relieve my neighbors.

It clearly makes sense to consider how cultural differences in gender roles might affect your research and happiness in the field before the field work begins.

Lest it appear that we are pointing only to the problems associated with bringing the family to the field, let us emphasize that aside from the obvious emotional benefits of having your spouse and children in the field, the family can help in practical aspects of research. For example, one of the coauthors benefited greatly from his wife's willingness to help in the research process by making telephone calls to set up interviews (often a time-consuming process) and collecting research materials from libraries. Another researcher found, much to his surprise, that his children's playmates helped him make important contacts through their parents or grandparents. Although obviously idiosyncratic, such accidents are probably more common than is typically assumed.

Academic Preparations

To this point we have been concerned with personal matters in preparation for the work in the field. While these issues are important, the primary task is clearly the actual research project. The final section of the chapter focuses on preparations for work.

The most general piece of advice offered by experienced field-workers is to contact as many researchers familiar with the site or subject as possible before going to the field. Contacts at your home institution (and elsewhere) can usually help in this regard, but do not be reluctant to make "cold" calls to experienced researchers to whom you have no third-party introduction. As one contributor pointed out,

> When I think of the useful advice to give someone leaving to conduct research in West Africa, I would emphasize the importance of developing contacts before departing. A means to begin is to contact scholars in the United States who have worked in that country. The Africanist community is not terribly large, and most people are pleased to help someone with names and addresses. Then, mailing follow-up notes will help establish cordial relations before arriving in the country. Such contacts are extremely important for conducting research and the people should be respected and included in any acknowledgments and on the mailing lists for subsequent publications.

Such advice is obviously not limited only to Africanists. Most research communities are relatively small, and many people in them are willing to help if asked, and should be acknowledged if they do.

At the same time you may encounter reluctance from veteran researchers for any of a variety of reasons. The veteran may find the intellectual project of a new researcher suspect. Or the experienced scholar may be reluctant to reveal names of sensitive contacts without first getting to know you and your project in more detail. This natural (and sensible) resistance should not be taken personally, nor is it necessarily a sign that the veteran researcher is not willing to help. As one researcher who has been asked for contacts puts it, "I do agree that people should seek out contacts in the U.S. who can help them, but they shouldn't have unrealistic expectations."

In the process of preparing academically, it is usually useful to establish contacts with a local research institution or university, as we discussed in Chapter 2. Such contact can facilitate access to libraries, local academics and contacts, photocopying facilities, and secretarial assistance. An institutional affiliation can also help you establish electronic communications, including access to the internet. Furthermore, such affiliations can often provide potential research assistants or enumerators, many of whom have invaluable research experience. Often the first step in arranging an affiliation is a formal, written request for support. One researcher recommends "securing an official letter of introduction (in a local language) from the president/chancellor of the home institution. In many parts of the world, nothing works better than official letterhead to assuage the obstructionist tendencies of a customs, government, or academic official."

Affiliations are not always what one hopes for, however. An institution's resources and personnel determine the value of affiliation to the researcher, as one pointed out: "I wrote a letter, cold, to an institution in Costa Rica which was kind enough to write back. But once I got there, they really only did two useful things for me: write me letters to help me renew my visa every three months, and give me a connection which helped with a very difficult situation of getting government data. These are no small things. They weren't what I expected but I sure did need them." You should have realistic, even if limited, expectations of what a local research institute can do, which is often a consequence of the limited resources that research institutes in many developing countries face.

In addition to making contacts in the field before departure, also make arrangements to keep in touch with researchers at home, whether your adviser (if you are a graduate student) or colleagues. Fortunately, the increasing spread of electronic mail is making this task easier than it was only a few years ago. Links to the internet are widely available through research institutes, universities, government offices, embassies, NGOs, or the increasing number of commercial online services available in many developing countries.

Maintaining contact with stateside researchers can prove important during the research process. Although some may want to return home during the fieldwork to take a break or check with advisers, this can prove financially burdensome if not covered by the basic research grant (or some other patron). If the return home is not easy, then being able to bounce an idea or a change in research focus off other academics or an adviser through e-mail or fax can prove invaluable. After all, your thinking about academic work tends to change while in the field—usually for the better—and if you are isolated from others who are, in effect, your audience, you can make serious mistakes and waste valuable fieldwork time. When collaborating with other researchers, such contact is all the more vital. Keep in mind also that some grantsmakers will want mid-stream progress reports, so knowing how they can be easily contacted via electronic mail or fax can save time and energy. In other words, we highly recommend planning ahead to make sure you will know how to get in touch with those who are important to your work.

A researcher often needs research clearance, or at least a research visa, before being allowed into the country. In some countries this can be difficult, especially if the researcher is investigating somewhat sensitive topics. The more authoritarian (or protective of information) the regime in power, the more difficult this may be. As one researcher who did his work in China noted,

> I really want to stress the difficulties confronting research in oppressed political systems. We tend to assume that we can go abroad and just collect data and conduct interviews. In essence, research is a messy process, especially when politics is involved. I adopted a "Chinese way" of conducting research through individual contacts rather than through the normal bureaucratic routes associated with the Commission of State Education. This commission has been known to hinder research by denying access to interviewees and research sites. My so-called Chinese way was to rely on contacts to gain inroads into realms not often traveled by foreign researchers.

Informal points of access are often crucial, especially in countries where the formal contacts are meant to place obstacles in the way of the researcher. Nevertheless, to navigate these waters, you should have a very thorough understanding of local politics. This knowledge can be expanded substantially through early and frequent contact with researchers who have been to the research site before.

The need for sensitivity to local politics is pronounced when seeking formal research clearance. As Karen Booth points out in the following narrative, even careful prior consideration of the politics of securing research clearance may miss important issues.

As Karen Booth demonstrates, many mistakes can occur in the process of "placing" yourself in a research context. Sometimes, the errors emerge from a misplaced or misunderstood sensitivity about what is and what is not acceptable in a particular country. As one researcher recounted, his eventual choice of institutional affiliation was inappropriate:

> I chose to establish a formal affiliation with an institution on the mistaken assumption that because of my research topic, which dealt with the business community, an affiliation with a

The Complications of Research Clearance

My process of securing research clearance in Kenya alternated between the hysterical and the banal and ended in anticlimactic success. The Kenyan government is infamous among American Africanist scholars for being exceptionally slow and unenthusiastic about granting research clearance. The process of getting clearance for AIDS research is, on the surface at least, even more difficult; the proposal has to be approved by a committee in the Ministry of Health and then by the President's office. When I told Africans in the know that I not only wanted to study policy in Kenya but that I was interested in prostitutes and AIDS, the modal response was something to the effect of: "you have got to be kidding; go to Uganda." Decidedly daunted but irrationally stubborn, I depoliticized my proposal by replacing all the references to prostitutes with the term women and all the references to sex with reproduction. I then sent it off to a politically savvy Kenyan friend. My friend sent it back saying it was still too controversial. So I depoliticized further by organizing the study around an apparently "technical" policy problem that the World Health Organization had already addressed, which had become part of the discourse in development and health circles in Kenya, and which fit with a mainstream, not inherently revolutionary, concern with "women and development."

I submitted this proposal to the AIDS committee, on the advice that I wait for their approval before allowing the President's office to see my ideas. My first mistake was to ask my friend to deliver the proposal to the committee. This was a faux pas on several levels. First, my friend was a peon within the hierarchy of the medical research bureaucracy; his low status reflected on me. Second, my friend was in the political bad graces of the head of the committee; his politics (with which I in fact agreed) made me suspect. Third, my friend was not affiliated with the project with which I requested to work; his role in my research was not clear to the committee—and mattered. In other words, the process or channel of communication was at least as important as the content of the proposal. Unwittingly I had repoliticized at an interpersonal level what I had taken such pains to depoliticize at an intellectual level.

I did not, however, discover that this was a large part of the reason that I had not heard anything on my proposal until I arrived in Kenya on a tourist visa. A number of people in the States had warned me not to go to Kenya without research clearance. My experience is evidence that this is not always the best policy. It was only when I was there, able to find out who really mattered in the committee, hand deliver my proposal, apologize profusely for my ignorant lack of protocol, and explain the nature of the study that I was able to get my proposal onto the committee's agenda and find a backer for it. This process occupied me for six weeks, during which time I was able to make some invaluable connections, understand the living situation in Nairobi, and have lots of unproductive panic sessions about how I could change my dissertation if I didn't get clearance. I handed over responsibility for the process to my Kenyan advisor and left to do the Geneva portion of my fieldwork, hoping optimistically to return fully cleared in three months.

In Geneva I heard nothing until I ran into my Kenyan advisor at a conference nearly three months later. She said that I would get my clearance in August. August came and I had heard nothing. I wrote to someone in Kenya who discovered that my proposal had not even been discussed by the committee. Enter hysteria. It was, obviously, time for dissertation plan B. I restructured my proposal, experienced an enormous amount of relief as well as regret and self-recrimination at the prospect of not doing the Nairobi fieldwork when I received in the mail in late September a very brief letter: the committee had approved the proposal and I should come to Nairobi to get the President's rubber stamp. I can't really describe the psychic impact of this turn of events. I had to do a total reversal in a day. I worried that I'd get back and still not get the President's approval and have my hands tied once again. I relived all the anxiety about entering the field and doing ethnography that I should have gotten over months before. And I went back. The first week I was there, I walked into the President's office and was given a research clearance paper after a half-hour wait.

KAREN BOOTH

more conservative institution would open more doors. This, I believe, turned out to be a poor criterion for choosing an institutional affiliation and instead I should have made a choice based on what institution would provide the greatest support for my research.

The lesson of this particular experience is not that political factors should not help determine your affiliation with a local institution; rather, your assumptions can often be wrong about those factors. Grasping what to do and making the appropriate contact for your particular research topic are not easy tasks, and figuring out the appropriate ways to approach the research task before going to the field can help to grease the wheels of research in many ways. Again, the advice to consult with others who have been to your particular "field" before merits reemphasis.

The preparation for the actual fieldwork is often the part of the research that produces the greatest amount of anxiety. Uncertainty is at its highest just before one hits the ground. In the next chapter we address the actual landing.

4

Setting Up to Live and Work

Having finally figured out where to go, you now have to plunge into the actual trip—a step fraught with apprehension. If this plunge has been preceded by a preparatory trip (see Chapter 2), established contacts and, hopefully, an understanding of the lay of the land at the research site will make the adjustment somewhat easier. Nevertheless, you do not usually know what to expect or have only a vague notion of possible problems. Even for those who have gone to the field on a preparatory research trip, preparing to do the actual research is often a chore. The early stages of research are most taxing, particularly because you do not know what to expect or, in many cases, what exactly you are doing.

Once arriving in the field, it might take you weeks to figure out how to live and work. In this chapter on the initial stages of field-work, we take a practical look at some of the main issues involved in the transition.

Becoming Familiar with an Unfamiliar Environment

Seasoned researchers commonly advise, "Don't expect to get much done during your first week or two." Above all, you will have to worry about practical things such as finding housing and arranging local finances. Taking care of such practical matters will demand most of your energy in the early stages. The difficulties associated with setting up in the field will depend on both how long you plan to stay and the particular research site. Although Gretchen Bauer's account (see below) is specific to Namibia, she offers some broader lessons to those who have just arrived.

As Bauer notes, it often helps to check out the local media in the process of settling into the research site. Reading newspapers, watch-

---

Taking the Time to Acclimate

I arrived in Namibia at the beginning of December—a real down period in that country. It is the hottest time of the year and generally during the Christmas and New Year's holidays, the country just shuts down and people travel outside of the cities and towns—to the coast or to the north of the country. But it was just as well to arrive at this time because it takes a considerable amount of time to settle in and to familiarize oneself and one should allow oneself that time. Do not feel that you can or should begin your research the day after you arrive in-country. It is very important to take the time to set up a household and familiarize oneself before embarking on the much more difficult research enterprise. Thus I spent a fair amount of time setting up a household—obtaining furniture and buying pots and pans and blankets and so on. Also, one needs to learn one's way around—to buy a map and locate different relevant sites, to find out about public transport if there is any. It might be important to locate places where one can exercise—a swimming pool or track, for example. Similarly, one needs to know where to shop for various things—groceries, office supplies, etc. Also, one should check out the local media—radio, newspapers, and television. These will undoubtedly be important sources of information in one's research and in one's daily living. The idea is to integrate oneself as fully as possible. Skipping over settling-in things or rushing through them can have negative consequences later on. As a rule I think the things to do are very much the same things that one would do in any new environment. If you know anyone at your research site—no matter how little you might know them—contact them. It is also imperative to begin meeting people as soon as possible.

GRETCHEN BAUER

---

ing television, or listening to the radio in-country can help in a couple of ways. In particular, it can improve your language ability, especially with local slang and colloquial expressions. It is also a very effective means of "getting inside" a local culture and political context. Attention to the media is one of the best ways to pick up the nuances and idiosyncrasies of any country or city or town.

Do not get frustrated at not being able to immediately jump into the research. Figuring out the right people to talk with is never easy, although a preparatory research trip certainly helps. Be patient at the beginning, realizing that much time will be taken up dealing with simply becoming situated.

Money and Housing

How do you take care of the practicalities of housing and money when in the field? Some of the relevant issues were addressed in the previous chapter on predeparture preparations. Nevertheless, you may want to make financial arrangements once in the field that make life easier. One of the options will be to set up a local bank account. Having a local bank account can make it much easier to pay bills and access money and is certainly safer than keeping money under the mattress, at least in many countries. The wisdom of setting up an account depends on the stability and reliability of the local financial system, as well as your location, the regulations placed on foreigners with bank accounts, and on the length of your stay in the field.

You will also want to investigate the possibility of transferring funds from abroad. This can be more difficult than you might imagine, so contact banks in the United States before you leave for the field. One of the advantages of establishing a local bank account is that you will often be able to make the international transfer of funds simpler if it becomes necessary to do so. You should also keep in mind that some credit card companies will allow the cardholder to purchase traveler's checks with a check written on a home bank account.

As for housing, one of the recommendations in the previous chapter was to have some provisional plans set up when arriving in the field. In many cases, such a temporary arrangement will last only a few days. Assuming that you do not find your ideal home immediately, you will want to consider short-term arrangements in an apartment or house. In some cities, short-term leases (of a month, for example) are possible and should be investigated. Moving to temporary quarters is likely to save a great deal of money, especially since an apartment or house is likely to have cooking facilities, thus sparing the expense of eating out.

In finding more permanent arrangements, keep in mind that many countries have bureaucratic or legal hoops that might seem strange. For example, one researcher pointed out that in Guatemala, "foreigners need to have a local person, usually someone who owns property, to cosign rental agreements." This can sometimes be circumvented by paying several months' rent in advance, or providing other "guarantees" of your moral and financial standing.

Field-experienced researchers suggest a wide variety of ways to find housing. One strategy that is probably more reliable in urban areas is to check the classified ads in the local newspaper(s). If nothing else, this provides some idea of rental prices. Another way to find appropriate housing in urban areas is through a local real estate agent specializing in rental properties. Embassies sometimes have a list of such agents. Depending on the country, you may have to pay an agency fee, either a fixed sum or a percentage of the first month's rent. Regardless of whether the landlord or renter pays the fee, you will probably pay more through an agent. One researcher advised: "I would be cautious about renting through an agent after only a few days of looking. I think it is best to use the agents to help gain familiarity with the city, but then to check the fairness of their prices by asking local friends or checking newspaper ads."

Finally, you can rely on informal networks to find housing, especially on the experience of researchers already in the field (perhaps you can occupy their dwelling when they leave). These informal networks become broader and more reliable with more field time. As one contributor put it, "We relied on the *South American Handbook* for travel and lodging information at first, but the longer we stayed, the more we relied on personal contacts and accumulated knowledge." If you are patient (for example, by finding a temporary dwelling that you can put up with for a month), you will be much more likely to find satisfactory housing, especially in a city. Informal networks and contacts are even more important in rural areas, where the housing market may be thin or weak.

Of course, what is satisfactory will depend on your circumstances and tastes. Most obviously, if you are alone, you may be willing to board with a family, as many single researchers do. Another scholar suggested teacherages, dormitories for teachers, as an option, noting

The Unexpected Living Arrangement

I arranged to rent a luxurious apartment in a high-rise Copacabana condo. The owners were an international buyer of bailer twine for a Minnesota agricultural cooperative and an offshore oilman working in Brazil for Zapata Oil (George Bush's former company). The buyer was a former Food for Peace worker in the 1960s; he gave up his humanitarianism but not his Brazilian contacts. The oilman was a former Peace Corps volunteer and AID field representative— a similar career trajectory. Both indulged heavily in the "exotic" aspects of Brazilian culture. The buyer even pictured himself as an American James Bond in Brazil (he admitted that his briefcase combination was 007). Thus, I found myself living in an apartment with beads hanging in doorways, mood lights, ceiling fans, and a waterbed built into the plushly carpeted bedroom floor. Despite my initial shock upon arriving at the apartment, I eventually grew quite fond of it. The owners, who visited occasionally, were interesting fellows who did have a lot of good advice about getting around in Rio. The rent for the apartment was a little higher than what I could have found elsewhere, but the place was secure, clean, and conveniently located.

TYLER PRIEST

that "some secondary schools are anxious to keep their teacherages rented to bring in income." Generally speaking, singles can settle for somewhat more unusual circumstances, as Tyler Priest's vivid account demonstrates.

With a family—and in particular with children—housing options are much more limited, and the search requires more patience. Many researchers found it useful to go to the field ahead of their families to secure permanent accommodations, since it can be tricky to search with a child in tow. Having some extra time to look for housing for the family can allow you to become familiar with local neighborhoods, schools, and day care centers. Going ahead of the family is particularly advisable when you need to find temporary accommodations, most of which would not suit a family.

Be wary of how locals perceive foreign researchers searching for housing. Although you are in a privileged position relative to most of the local population, most fieldworkers are not as rich as potential landlords may believe. As one scholar observed, "The highly competitive nature of the [housing] market and the belief on the part of many real estate agents that my pockets were stuffed with money made the search for an apartment a real nightmare." Such an experience is not at all unusual; be prepared for it. Research grants will not support the kinds of accommodations embassy personnel rent, but many locals will not differentiate between senior diplomats and graduate students.

An entirely separate and important issue concerns the interaction between your living arrangements and your research. Some research designs effectively dictate active involvement in the observed community. For example, it is hard to imagine fieldwork in social anthropology in which the researcher does not live smack in the middle of the subject population, often with a local family. Your choice of lodging can erect or reduce social barriers between you and the locals. In some cultures, for instance, reciprocity is important, and an outsider living on her own, reasonably self-sufficiently, may be perceived as unintegrated into the complex local web of interdependence and thus as untrustworthy.

Bureaucratic and Legal Matters

In the previous chapter we discussed issues regarding research clearance and the necessity of delegating power of attorney at home. Here we address only the bureaucratic and legal matters you will likely confront in-country. Even if you received research clearance, there are often still bureaucratic hurdles to clear. In particular, you may have to register with the police or another internal security agency, often to receive a resident identity card or as a condition of research clearance. This is common not only in countries with authoritarian regimes; many countries are interested in keeping track of the doings of foreign researchers. Embassies are also interested in knowing the whereabouts of visiting nationals and can provide valuable services in case of an emergency. So it is wise to register with your embassy as well.

Some countries are also particularly concerned with what foreigners bring in for research purposes. Most problems occur over research equipment such as laptop computers. In many cases, after some paperwork, a research visa makes it relatively easy to bring in needed equipment. Keep in mind that the chief concern of trade bureaucracies is that you might sell the imported equipment illegally, thereby undermining local customs laws. We return to these issues in Chapter 5.

In addition, you may need to deal with the local immigration department to renew a visa or to change your visa status. Needless to say, this can be a frustrating experience, or, for one contributor, almost a surreal one:

> I can say without exaggeration that I went through over two dozen different trips to different government offices and ministries, and all of that without any objection or opposition to my request for renewal of my visa. It was simply a Kafkaesque experience of being sent from one functionary to another, each of whom added to the list of requirements or claimed that I had come to the wrong place. At one point, when an official told me that I had come to the wrong office, even though an official in a different ministry insisted that that was where I was supposed to go, and told me instead to go to a ministry across town, I asked if he was certain. He replied that I had offended him by doubting him. So I dutifully went off to the ministry to which he directed me, only to be told that I had gone to the wrong place and was sent somewhere else.

Faced with such situations, you may be tempted to offer a bribe to an obstructing official. After all, many researchers carry to the field a stereotype of the relatively corrupt developing country official, and might figure that a few well-placed bills will grease the bureaucratic wheels and allow them to get on with their work. This stereotype is often inaccurate and the strategy is perilous, in both ethical and practical terms. We strongly recommend against attempts at bribery. Even if such practices seem common in the host country, foreigners rarely know what they are doing; bribery is, after all, a rather complicated cultural practice. Bribery carries with it real risks. A foreigner with substantial resources who breaks the law is an easy target. You may consider yourself savvy in offering a bribe, but usually you are simply being stupid.

With Family in the Field

As noted in the previous chapter, going to the field with the family poses special challenges. A number of the important issues regarding family in the field were tackled in Chapter 3, so here we briefly address one issue in particular: finding day care or schools for children in the field.

If accompanied to the field by children, you almost certainly have to arrange for day care, schooling, or both. Although it is difficult to arrange these from abroad, try to do so if at all possible. One researcher with a small child pointed out that although you might be reluctant to place a child in day care when abroad, it can provide the child with some continuity if he or she is already used to a day care environment. It may also be necessary when both parents are working on research and/or writing. A number of researchers pointed out that some sort of home day care is often feasible, although it might be difficult to get used to the idea of having domestic help.

Indeed, while many researchers instinctively feel uncomfortable employing domestic help, there are several reasons to do so. The first is time. "If you always cook for yourself," observed one contributor, "you might be taking valuable time away from your work. I tried to cook for myself at first, but the challenges of transforming food from its unprocessed form to something nutritious and edible in one pot proved to be too much for me. I eventually hired a young girl to come and cook in the evenings for me, which enabled me to get in a good three hours more of research time." The second reason to hire domestic help is employment creation. Whether or not you deplore the economic structure that leads to a large class of unemployed and underemployed in your research site, refusing to employ domestic help on "moral" grounds neither changes that structure nor provides jobs to those who need them.

Setting up schooling for children quite naturally makes parents uneasy. One seasoned researcher noted that he and his wife took quite a bit of time at the beginning of his research period to find an appropriate school for their first-grader. They ended up visiting more than half a dozen schools before settling on one. A number of factors entered into their decision-making process, including cost, the language spoken in the school, and the quality of the education. As for cost, bear in mind that schools for foreigners are often prohibitively expensive for the researcher on a limited budget. Many of these schools cater to the children of foreign diplomats and international businesspersons, most of whose employers pay for their children's education. You should think seriously about the language in which classes will be taught. Some will prefer schools that teach in English, so as to ease the transition for the child. At the same time, the cost of English-speaking schools is usually greater. The quality of educational systems in most developing countries varies greatly (often more so than it does at home). More often than not, foreign researchers enroll their children in private schools abroad.

Finally, be aware that the adjustment to a new school in a new country with a new language can be extremely difficult for a child. Be alert to the stress that it might cause for your child. As one researcher pointed out, at the beginning of the research period the child may be unable to handle many things previously taken for granted, for example, the ability to cope with the cruelties that children inevitably inflict on one another. Like adults, children often feel defenseless if they cannot verbalize. So, consider some elementary language lessons for your child before going to the field.

Issues of Gender, Race, Class, and Age

Gender, race, class, and age have a profound effect on both setting up in the field and in the actual fieldwork itself. Simply put, people react differently to men and women, to persons of different skin color, and to older and younger researchers, and the quality of your research will be affected by the differences in response.

Being a woman can sometimes help when doing fieldwork. In the words of one female researcher, "I found that my gender role actually helped my research experience—as a woman, people saw me as less threatening than a male researcher." Such perceptions of women are probably common in many countries and, however misplaced, can be used to advantage. In a similar vein, both men and women in the research site will likely feel that the single woman alone needs "protection and assistance," which can often prove valuable in practical terms during the rigors of fieldwork, as a number of women contributors pointed out.

There are, of course, distinct disadvantages to being a woman in the field. Some of these disadvantages are personal; others are academic. Women often have to deal with harassment, and as one scholar who did her work in Latin America pointed out, "women who are not from

Los Angeles or New York have to get used to the way men are expected to hiss at women in the street." This same researcher also noted wryly that single women in particular can have problems finding housing: "People are reluctant to rent to single females, especially North Americans, because [they say] we have no morals." Needless to say, the power of stereotypes, especially in an era of internationally syndicated TV dramas, is often difficult to overcome, especially in cultures where one is an outsider.

Professionally and academically, gender can affect one's access to informants. As one researcher reported, "When I told [male] agronomists that I was doing my work on women in agriculture, they invariably steered me towards the widows, as if these were the only category of women working in agriculture." Similarly, a male researcher may be encouraged to talk only to men, which can obviously bias research conclusions, or, if he is trying to study work that women do, he may face different obstacles. One male scholar noted that because he was doing research on household economic practices and would need to interview mainly women, he found it necessary and useful to hire a female research assistant and female enumerators once in the field. These circumstances are hardly unusual. It is essential to remain aware that gender frequently influences the kind and source of information that is provided. As another scholar noted, "It would be hard to conceive of a research topic in which gender did not matter somehow. . . . Male and female perceptions and experiences of similar things are frequently very different, and one rarely can have a complete and full picture without interviewing people of both sexes."

Some women noted how gender interacts with race to produce unexpected outcomes about which other women should be aware. Laura Hammond discusses her experience in the field narrative opposite.

The disadvantages of gender are sometimes neutralized by the advantages of race and class. As one woman put it, "Being a foreign woman tends to protect one in those instances where [native] women might be discriminated against or disadvantaged." The particular research site and topic will determine the degree to which disadvantages can be offset or turned into advantages. As another researcher pointed out, "It is of course difficult to tease out the effects of gender from those of race, nationality, and class in assessing my experiences in the field. Equally it is impossible to know if and how I might have been treated differently if I were a man."

Gender, Race, and the Outside Researcher

It is difficult to say whether my gender helped me in my efforts to settle in. I suppose it did, for I was a single woman, on my own, and therefore by the conventions of Tigrayan [Ethiopian] society I was in need of protection and assistance. On the other hand, I am not convinced that some of the villagers ever really considered me to be fully female. To many I think I was sort of a nongendered creature. One woman even grabbed my breasts to see if I really had any! Many people could not understand how I could have reached the age of twenty-seven without having gotten married or had children. As a white woman I could balance both gender roles. I could interview men in the houses where local beer was brewed and sold, places forbidden to respectable women, but I could also sit with women in their homes and discuss intimate aspects of childbirth, a subject which was off-limits to men. As I got to know people better, they came to accept me as having definite differences from Tigrayan women, but as female nonetheless.

LAURA HAMMOND

Most researchers also confront class differences. While most graduate student researchers feel far from rich when conducting fieldwork, they are usually better off than the vast majority of the population where they are studying, which, one researcher pointed out, warrants special sensitivity:

In some cultures, this status implies certain expectations of reciprocity and generosity that one should familiarize oneself with. People may sometimes have certain expectations of you that may be unrealistic, but necessitate some gestures that indicate that you are not oblivious to them. . . . Even though students may not feel that they are "rolling in the dough," they often are not fully aware of how wealthy they are in comparison to many of their counterparts in their host country.

Indeed, academics in many developing countries must live with uncertainty about job stability, and in many countries they have to hold down several jobs to make ends meet. Sensitivity to this reality makes the research process smoother and more productive.

Finally, the age of the researcher and local assumptions about what is expected of people of a particular age affect access to informants and social treatment. Like class and race, age can neutralize the disadvantages of gender in many cultures. One female researcher, discussing sexual harassment, made observations and suggested strategies "to minimize these unpleasant interactions": "The older you are, the less prone you are to such abuses. . . . The more 'professional,' businesslike, and mature [-looking] your clothes, the less likely you are to evoke such reactions."

More generally, female researchers must get used to the fact that they will often be viewed as suspect because of their chosen career path. Indeed, Hammond's descriptions (above) demonstrate the effects not only of race and gender, but age as well. She points out that she was considered an oddity because she had not gotten married nor had children by the ripe old age of twenty-seven. As another scholar observed in this regard, "In the United States, grad students often have to postpone marriage and children for the sake of their studies or they may choose not to marry or have children for various reasons. Yet these life choices may be regarded with suspicion among people one is working with abroad. . . . I have observed how a lack of sensitivity to these age grades and life experiences can at times lead to serious breakdowns in communication." Strategies for coping with these inevitable differences include observing the behavior of others very carefully, and asking locals with whom you feel comfortable (friends of a similar age, your language instructor) about proper etiquette.

Relations with Expatriates

At some point in the research (often at the beginning), you will be confronted with the presence, social opportunities, and demands of expatriates in the field. There are no hard and fast rules or advice to give when one deals with fellow foreigners. The experiences of researchers overseas with expatriate communities varies widely.

On the positive side, expatriates can be useful for making contacts in the field—both social and academic—and these contacts are usually most useful in the early stages of research. Other scholars in your field can help with "seasoned" information regarding contacts, housing, financial matters, potential informants, local research institutions, and local libraries or archives. Foreign researchers can also help you test ideas in the formative stage, since fellow researchers are usually familiar with academic cultures at home. Contact with expatriates can also come in handy when sending correspondence or light packages home. Many expatriates returning home, on leave or permanently, quite willingly serve as couriers.

Contacts with expatriates can also help in the logistics of fieldwork. One scholar's contacts with other foreign researchers helped to determine how and how much to pay research team members, a reasonable work schedule, and where to recruit potential research team members. Contact with other foreigners doing research in the field also provides information on what others are doing, which can provide for intellectual stimulation and is a way to avoid the potential disaster of duplicating another's research.

Finally, on a social level, befriending other expatriates can offer some balance to life during an intense period. One colleague noted that while most of his friends in the field were local, he and his wife found it possible to "let their hair down" with a good friend who hailed from the United States. Contact with those from your own culture can provide a needed and helpful break from the grind of fieldwork and a soothing cultural touchstone.

There are, nonetheless, drawbacks to spending a lot of time with foreigners in the field. While socializing with expatriates can help, one contributor remarked that "to alleviate the inevitable sense of isolation, . . . ex-pat communities tend to be clannish, incestuous, hived-off from local society—to exhibit all the characteristics of very small towns." You will have many fewer opportunities to immerse yourself in local culture and language if you hang out with expatriates too much.

When it comes to dealing with other segments of the expatriate society—officials at the embassy or foreign aid missions, for example— most researchers recommend some distance. One wrote, "I tried to stay away from the Embassy folks as much as possible. They are a very insular group; those who live in the embassy compound usually do not go out very often, and they generally haven't spent much time in the rest of the country." Below, Gretchen Bauer sums up a feeling expressed by a number of researchers. There are good reasons to be careful of relationships with expatriate communities, especially when they are "official."

Bear in mind Bauer's point that researchers with U.S. government funds may need the official community for things such as visa re-

Relationships with Expatriate Communities

I think it can be a real trap to associate too strongly with any of the expatriate communities. They tend to live in considerable isolation from the people of the country and yet believe they know what is going on because they talk to their domestic workers, gardeners, drivers, and other employees. While the old suspicions toward Americans, and especially anyone associated with the official community, seem to have waned somewhat, efforts to live among the people of a country rather than with fellow expatriates are enormously appreciated and certainly infinitely more rewarding for the researcher. At the same time, one must tread carefully. Especially if one has U.S. government funds (e.g., as a Fulbright scholar) one must learn what is expected by the embassy or U.S. Information Service office and must certainly avoid antagonizing anyone. I think cordial but cool relations can be the best unless, of course, one wants more. A drawback of associating with the Embassy or USIS people is that they, recognizing their own dearth of information, may attempt to get more information from those researchers they know to be well-acquainted with the local scene. Here it is especially important not to betray any confidences of one's respondents. The official community hires its own people to obtain information and they should not be after researchers—even those from their country—for such input.

GRETCHEN BAUER

newal, use of the diplomatic pouch, or access to the embassy health clinic. Thus, be careful not to alienate those who provide such services. It should also be noted that researchers report a rather wide variety of experiences with expatriate officials. Some can be extraordinarily helpful, others can be mostly a hindrance. Whatever the specific circumstances, exercise some caution in your dealings with officials.

Finally, a comment on expatriates by a scholar who has worked in North Africa captures some of the ways in which such communities can provide another perspective:

I have found U.S. expatriates to be some of the most bizarre, eccentric, and, therefore, entertaining people I have ever met. They're always weird or unique in some way. We enjoyed socializing with Americans, sharing ideas, arguing, drinking. Government folks—USIS, USAID, American Embassy—were especially interesting to spend time with. They were sources of information, and it was fascinating to listen to their views of Tunisia and Tunisians. Many of them, shall we say, live in an enclave. They had guards and drivers, they shopped at the commissary, they avoided learning Arabic. Yet they had ample opinions about Tunisians. It was interesting to observe their behavior.

However you choose to approach the expatriate community—as an obstacle, a source of support, or an object of study—expatriates are just one small part of a fascinating puzzle.

Maintaining Sanity in the Field

The field work experience is almost always intense, and can be trying as you attempt to get used to a new environment while concurrently working at breakneck speed. Resources and time are limited, and so you may be tempted to work all of the time so as to not let opportunities slip by. Nevertheless, almost all experienced field researchers highly recommend taking regular breaks. A vacation can be rejuvenating and often makes you more productive in the long term. As one researcher put it, "Before I started my fieldwork, I had a vision of staying in my field site for months and months at a time," but this vision soon gave way to the real need for breaks. This researcher went on to note that "I used to feel guilty about taking these breaks. I felt that I wasn't a real anthropologist unless I was in the thick of it all the time. Finally I made peace with the fact that I needed the breaks and that I work better if I can get out for a while. I come back refreshed, often with new ideas, and with new enthusiasm for the research." Another researcher recommended taking a vacation around the middle of the research trip, since it often becomes increasingly difficult to break away near the end of the stay. One of the coauthors is grateful to his wife for making him take a few weekend trips near the end of the research period. Some occasional cooling off is needed when running at full tilt, as inevitably occurs deep into your field time.

It is especially important for people who are on their own to take the occasional break from work. You might be even more tempted to work all of the time when alone and anxious to return home to loved ones, but it is not advisable. The absence of a companion with whom to share ideas often discourages critical reflection on the research experience in progress. Moreover, the fatigue of incessant work only worsens the emotional challenges faced by a homesick fieldworker. A break can be of even greater value under such circumstances.

Many researchers pointed out the importance of exercise in the field. Several problems crop up as you attempt to keep up a regular exercise routine in the field. The most important limitation is the dearth of facilities. Northern researchers grow accustomed to universities with excellent athletic facilities for which they do not have to pay, at least explicitly. Such arrangements are highly unusual in most developing countries. More often than not, the only good facilities are private clubs costing a small fortune, beyond the typical researcher's financial means. You may have to come up with alternatives to gym facilities for exercise. If you run regularly, pay attention to personal safety. Even if you have to be concerned about personal safety at home, you are also much more familiar with your home environment. Driving habits, the conditions of roads, sidewalks and the air, leashing and vaccination of dogs, and other environmental differences can affect the running experience (sometimes dramatically). Biking and swimming are sometimes popular and financially feasible options, although health and safety cautions still pertain.

Finally, several scholars noted the importance of writing—letters or a journal—as a way to release tension and gain insight into the research process. As one put it, "I enjoy writing and also receiving letters . . . I shared experiences and newspaper clippings and a few things from Thailand with my family and friends at home. They responded in kind, and as I have looked back over the correspondence I can see that it is really very hard to separate personal from professional issues in international research." Writing letters provides an opportunity to reflect on the research experience and can help in the process of discernment of research strategies and accomplishments.

Settling In Academically

To this point, we have been concerned with very practical issues of settling in to do research. Nonetheless, after the initial settling in period, you must figure out how to get on with work. This can be difficult, charting unknown territory on your own, often doing original research for the first time. In this last section, we discuss some of the ways in which you can get moving productively.

First, a few words on protocol and personal comportment. One of the most offensive things you can do is to arrive on site and begin making demands on local academic institutions, for example, demanding immediate access to electronic mail, office space, or secretarial services. One researcher notes that "the researcher should exercise some cultural sensitivity. Quiet observation may avert errors that can be costly to a researcher. In many countries in West Africa, personal relations are critical for the success or failure of a project. Warm greetings, remembering to ask about families, and immersing oneself in the culture may allow for a truly productive research experience." The importance of personal relations extends far beyond West Africa. As this researcher pointed out, common courtesy and sensitivity to the local way of doing things can be both personally and professionally rewarding. Keep in mind that "cold professionalism" is not necessarily appropriate, as it often is at home. This does not mean that you should spend all of your time on small talk, but it does mean that jumping straight into academic discussions can turn people off. The best way to figure out what is and is not appropriate is to listen and observe when you first arrive in the field.

Above all, most seasoned researchers counsel patience in the early stages of research. You will not get everything done immediately. You will likely go down more than a few dead-end paths. Becoming familiar with the ins and outs of a particular research context takes time; there is often no way to rush the process. Many scholars fear that not much is being accomplished during the beginning stages of the research. This is normal. Do not become unnecessarily alarmed.

If you arranged affiliation with a research institution before going to the field, one of the first things to do after arriving in-country is to visit the institution. As we noted in the previous chapter, the benefits of affiliation can vary greatly, from an office and secretarial support to an affiliation in name only. If at all possible, attempt to become involved in the institutional life early in the process of doing research. One scholar became immediately and actively involved in her research institute. Indeed, she ended up organizing a weekly seminar series on research in progress by the host institute's researchers and had a very positive experience with the affiliate.

Others are not so lucky, and find involvement in institutional life practically impossible. Some places do not have much of an institutional life. As one researcher pointed out: "My research affiliation and relations with the (few) Honduran scholars did not progress as anticipated. I found not [a single] student or professor who was really interested in my topic or anxious for research collaboration or shared authorship of an article."

If you have not set up an affiliation with a local research institution before going to the field, you should still visit the local institutions to make contacts. This is an appropriate courtesy to extend to professional colleagues. Moreover, such contacts often prove beneficial, especially when made early enough in the research period to make good use of them.

If you intend to use local libraries and archives, visit as many of these places as possible in the early stages of research. Establish what is and is not available, during what hours, and on which days. Try to determine which places are likely to have more useful information and deserve further exploration. Talk to the librarians or archivists at these institutions to find out what might be available that is not necessarily obvious. Unless you stumble onto a gold mine in the early stages of research, it is probably not advisable to spend too much time in any one place initially. Those who adopt a narrowing strategy too soon often later come to regret their blinders. Getting a broad lay of the land can help you feel productive and figure out what is available, and can help the process of narrowing and refining the research project early on.

Finally, a good and generalizable piece of advice offered by a researcher who spent two years in the field is to get to know as many people as possible: "I decided very early on that it was important that I first meet as many people as possible socially and that these social acquaintances could later be transformed into working relationships. I also realized early on that it would be quite some time before I felt in a position to conduct personal interviews, which meant that I had the time to spend in cultivating these relationships first." Not everyone will have the luxury of a long period of fieldwork, but it is important to keep in mind that any trip may be the first of many. Concern yourself with cultivating personal relationships for the long run.

5

The Logistics of Fieldwork

Some experienced field researchers suggest, with a mixture of amusement and exasperation, that fieldwork is one part intellectual exploration and ten parts daily maintenance. Even in the security of your home university, you inevitably spend far more time handling administrative details, financial matters, minor and major crises concerning computers or other necessary equipment, and personal and familial arrangements than is anticipated or desired. When displaced to a foreign culture, nonacademic demands on time multiply. More rudimentary communications and transportation infrastructure, unfamiliar legal and administrative procedures, and the challenges of working in a foreign language often seem to rob overseas field researchers of the time they need to get on with the study. This is a universal experience, for which the best advice is to be flexible and patient. However, knowing how others have handled common problems and with what results may be helpful to the daily maintenance of you and your project.

In this chapter we confront the myriad logistical issues involved in establishing and executing a field research project overseas. Few will need to consider all the subsidiary issues addressed here. Indeed, a fortunate minority will not concern themselves with computers, vehicles, or other materials, nor will they need research assistants. But the vast majority of researchers confront such issues, and many devise ingenious solutions to the challenges they encounter. Although these challenges sometimes prove exasperating, they are also an important, even potentially enjoyable part of the research process. As one scholar put it, "A sense of humor is very important. When I complained to a Moroccan friend that I had trouble with local, dialectal Arabic and Berber, she responded that people will always help you—despite language and cultural barriers—if they sense kindness, humor, and honesty."

Research Equipment

Although social science research, especially fieldwork, rarely demands elaborate laboratories filled with expensive and delicate equipment, even the simplest research designs today depend on some basic tools: computers, tape recorders, cameras, photocopiers, and the like. You need to think through the necessary equipment at an early stage, determine whether it is better to bring needed items along or to acquire them on site, and plan for maintenance.

Most field researchers consider a computer essential. A computer undoubtedly makes the research process more organized and efficient. As one researcher notes emphatically, you "should be writing in a journal or keeping regular notes constantly, every free minute you have. If it is inputted into the computer, this saves many hours [later], since you can, through various search methods, find key words and files in seconds once you start writing up." You can code, enter, clean, and even analyze data in the field, permitting followup correctives when necessary. Having a computer also helps begin the process of writing, and many experienced researchers think starting to write while still in the field is a good idea.

Equipment size and portability matters. A laptop computer is generally superior to a larger portable since you can take a laptop to field sites, libraries, or the office of a local contact or collaborator. Also, laptops are generally better suited to the less reliable electricity supplies of developing countries. If the power fails, most laptops automatically switch to battery power, and many have rudimentary surge protection built in as well. As one respondent put it, "I don't know how people used to do field research without laptops."

Opinions vary on what peripherals to bring along. It can be very difficult to locate, much less gain access to, functioning computer printers in many low-income countries. Thus, many researchers take portable computer printers to the field. Lightweight bubble inkjet types are especially popular among field researchers. One noted, "Although computers are widespread in the Philippines, decent printers are not always easy to find. Having one allows me some autonomy and to reserve asking favors for other needs." But at least one researcher took a printer that caused her considerable mechanical difficulty and proved to be just added weight and hassle. Others found their printing needs minimal and access to borrowed printers sufficient. Nonetheless, we concur with most scholars who recommend taking a printer to the field.

One political scientist doing archival work in Chile stumbled across several thousand pages of valuable documents that he was not permitted to photocopy and for which he wanted the text, not just notes. Fortunately, he was able to borrow a hand-held scanner from another foreign researcher. "The results were amazing. In a week and a half I had all the documents entered into my computer and printed out in hard copy." Indeed, the archivists were so impressed with the results that they set about obtaining a scanner for the library. For those doing much archival work, a scanner may be a worthwhile investment (although note that they have considerable memory requirements).

There is no simple rule as to whether or not to take computer peripherals. Consider your likely needs for printing, scanning, modem communications; the availability of such peripherals on site; and the costs of carrying, maintaining, and protecting the equipment. Then make a decision appropriate to the circumstances of the research project. If you do take peripherals, assemble and test the whole system at the home institution, if possible. This can facilitate identification and resolution of hardware or software conflicts that can bedevil fieldwork. One researcher lamented that because he did not buy and test his computer and printer together before leaving the United States, a small software problem that could have been corrected in a matter of minutes at home took several months to solve in Uganda.

Other equipment that contributing researchers mentioned as particularly useful included cameras, video cameras and monitors (for making a visual record of sites and events), microtape recorders and dictaphone machines (for taping and transcribing interviews), and scales (for anthropometric data collection). The needs of any particular project clearly vary with the work style of the researcher, the question at hand, and the environment in which the study is conducted.

The decision of whether to bring equipment along or to buy it on site generally turns on three issues: the relative price of the item(s) at home and in the host country, and your access to funds with which to make equipment purchases before departure; differences in the quality of equipment available in the different locations; government or grantsmaker restrictions on cross-border movement of equipment, and cross-cultural differences in equipment design. In all but a very few cases, equipment is cheaper, of better quality, and of greater variety in North America or Europe than in low- or middle-income countries, and is legally transportable across borders. Thus, most researchers take their equipment with them.

With some notable exceptions, most low- and middle-income countries import consumer electronics (e.g., computers, typewriters, cameras, tape recorders), so such items cost more in the host country than at home. The price differentials are sometimes dramatic, especially where foreign exchange flows are restricted or the government imposes heavy import tariffs on luxury items. No matter how necessary it might seem to the itinerant social scientist, most of the world still considers a laptop computer a luxury.

Check to see what restrictions the host country customs service places on items brought in. Some countries suspect that imported luxuries, such as computers, will be sold in-country and, thus, tax them as imports. These duties can be enormous. If there is no duty, there may well be restrictions on subsequent sale. Talk with researchers recently in-country or with embassy officials before your departure. It is often handy to have proof of purchase and a letter from some official body (e.g., a funding agency, host, or home institution) indicating that the equipment is for research purposes only and will not be sold.

Since purchasing power is limited in poorer countries, selection is often very limited for items such as laptop computers and microtape recorders. Also, the quality of available models may not meet your expectations or needs. Given price and quality differences, in most cases it seems far more cost-effective to take along necessary advanced research equipment than to purchase items on site.

This discussion also raises the broader question of product price/quality tradeoffs. Inexperienced field researchers too often err on the side of sacrificing necessary quality in an effort to conserve scarce funds. This often comes back to haunt them, as Dan Maxwell points out (see opposite).

Some grantsmakers (e.g., the U.S. government) insist or strongly suggest equipment purchases be made at home prior to departure. Your decision of where to purchase necessary equipment might thus be made by a third party. There can also be the matter of cross-cultural differences in equipment design. For example, if you need a computer that will be used by an assistant unfamiliar with European script, the appropriate equipment may be easier and cheaper to acquire on site than in Europe or North America. In a similar spirit, one contributor doing anthropometric surveying "purchased a very accurate scale for body weight in the U.S. and shipped it to Swaziland. It would have been far easier on me and the poor scale to have gotten it in South Africa. It was eventually donated to the Ministry of Agriculture and Coops [per donor guidelines on disposal of durable equipment] but since it was in pounds, not grams, its usefulness for them is somewhat dubious. A good example of a bad guess!"

Keep in mind that all equipment requires maintenance, some of which will inevitably exceed your abilities. Mechanical difficulties can drain your time, patience, and funds if your location lacks parts or technicians. For that reason, brand choice can be important. Unless you are working in urban areas of technologically advanced countries, it is wise to establish which manufacturers have service representatives, warranty repair facilities, and parts suppliers reasonably

---

Price/Quality Tradeoffs in Critical Equipment

I took a small tape recorder that I had bought in a dime store, not really thinking through what I was going to need it for. In the end, my research assistant and I struggled through hundreds of hours of interviewing and transcribing using this very substandard equipment mainly because I tried to take a $75 shortcut on the purchase of a decent tape recorder—a very big mistake.

Even on simple things, it is not worth trying to save a few dollars. I didn't want to take my good stapler, for example, because I thought I might lose it. So I bought the best I could get locally, and was never able to staple together more than six or seven sheets of paper—again, not a large frustration, but I had to assemble 720 fifteen-page questionnaires over the course of three months with a lousy stapler that didn't work. The examples go on and on, but the message should be simple: Don't cut corners on basic necessary equipment.

DAN MAXWELL

proximate to your research site. Several scholars bought a particular make of computer expressly because of service availability in the research site. Remember that many warranties are voided if an unauthorized technician services the equipment.

That said, the quality of the service ultimately depends on the local staff, who might not be well trained, well compensated, or highly motivated. The physical presence of a licensed warranty service center does not mean they can or will actually fix your equipment there. It is wise to clarify the terms of the warranty in advance and bring along the necessary documentation. But be forewarned that even reputable companies such as Hewlett Packard and Kodak do not always honor warranties overseas. In this era of faxes and electronic mail, however, you can almost always contact technical support or customer service at home if local technicians cannot solve the problem.

Be prepared with spare parts or even spare equipment. One researcher's pocket tape recorder was stolen in Namibia and she had to buy a second one at a substantially higher price.

Parts and supplies for equipment, if available at all, are often quite a bit more expensive overseas and of substantially lower quality. For example, twelve of a pack of twenty floppy diskettes purchased in Madagascar (at two to three times North American prices) failed within three months, while all twenty diskettes brought from the U.S. functioned flawlessly for a year or more. Even simple things, such as the right size staples for a foreign-made stapler or a replacement bulb for a flashlight, might not be available locally. Prepare for dust, heat, humidity, and rain. A small canister of compressed air, a soft brush, and some cotton rags (kept dry and clean in sealed plastic bags) can keep a laptop computer functioning for months or years in even the worst of conditions.

Security is as much a problem as maintenance, as the unusual case in the field narrative opposite illustrates. Petty larceny is widespread in many places and computers, cameras, and tape recorders are prized targets. Several commentators strongly recommended some form of antitheft device, if only a simple lock and chain. It is also wise to establish whether your renter's or homeowner's insurance policy covers equipment, especially computers, that might be damaged or stolen overseas. Many companies offer special computer endorsements as additional coverage at low cost.

Computer viruses can pose a special and severe problem to computer users in developing countries. Perhaps because so much software is pirated, viruses seem unusually commonplace outside Europe and North America. Buy a current copy of a good antivirus software, use it faithfully, and be cautious about introducing others' disks into your computer. In a similar vein, be religious about backing up your valuable and irreplaceable material. Such backups can be electronic, hard copy, or both. Also, bring computer startup disks, which can be extremely useful when software or hardware conflicts occur that prevent the computer from booting up when all the extensions and/or drivers are loaded.

Computers and Security

Because of [the Israeli airline's] price and flexibility, I flew to Kenya on El Al. . . . Obviously, El Al has enormous security concerns and a very elaborate and complete surveillance system. When I arrived at New York's JFK airport, I was questioned fully by El Al personnel. I was asked where I packed my bags and if anyone could have gained access to them. With supreme naivete I told them cheerfully that I had packed them in the home of a friend. I gave my friend's name before I remembered that this was obviously the name of a person of Lebanese descent. That did it. My computer, along with my tape recorder and iron, were confiscated and held in New York while I was given an armed escort to the plane just as it was about to take off. I did not see my computer for four weeks and spent a part of every day at the offices of El Al in Nairobi forcing them to search for this machine. Finally it was discovered that El Al had sent it to the Nairobi airport but had not bothered to let anyone know it was there. In the end I did get my computer and was able to catch up on my work.

I came full circle with my computer experience in the field when four weeks before I was to leave . . . my computer was stolen from my hotel room. I left as I arrived: without computer. The only moral to this story is that one should avoid becoming entirely dependent on a computer and try to anticipate that most things that can go wrong, will!

KAREN BOOTH

Good surge protection and power conditioning are likewise crucial for any sensitive electronics. This includes not just computers, but electrical typewriters, video monitors, and other equipment. Electrical grids in low-income countries are generally far less reliable than in Europe or North America, and power spikes and drains can corrupt data and software or permanently damage sensitive equipment. Know the voltage both for your electronics and for the outlets at your site. Many laptop computers and printers today switch automatically between 110 and 220 volts. This very desirable feature has saved more than one jet-lagged researcher from frying his computer when he unthinkingly took a unit last plugged into a 110-volt system and connected it directly to a 220-volt source. A power strip surge protector or, better yet, an uninterruptible power supply (UPS) can save equipment from debilitating surges.

Most researchers bring an extra battery pack or two for laptops or other mobile electronics. A remote battery charger can be helpful, too. In especially isolated locations, look into solar panels or power sources that plug into a vehicle cigarette lighter, or learn how to rig a recharger from a vehicle battery. Brownouts/blackouts commonly last far beyond the several hours of protection afforded by a couple of battery packs, so do not be surprised by downtime even when you have taken precautions.

Although it may seem obvious, take the time to establish the type of electrical plugs on your equipment and the wall sockets at your site and the appropriate adaptor(s). One of the coauthors failed to notice that his laptop computer had a three-flanged plug, and he brought only two-pronged adaptors. No shop on site carried the necessary adaptor, so he finally called the U.S. and had two seventy-five-cent adaptors sent by a delivery service. It cost sixty dollars and took two weeks, during which time the computer's batteries were, of course, completely exhausted. It later turned out that the U.S. Postal Service's Express Mail service could have delivered the same items in four days at one-quarter the price! So it pays not only to carefully check the details of your equipment, but also to shop around for the most inexpensive and timely means by which to resupply from home, since almost everyone forgets or loses something crucial that cannot be replaced in the field.

Most researchers engage in some photocopying, be it of archival materials, notes, or questionnaires. When doing bulk work (e.g., copying questionnaires for a large formal survey), it often pays to arrange a quantity discount with a single vendor. This can provide quicker, cheaper, and more reliable service than just walking in off the street. Also, be aware that copy quality is often poor.

Since all fieldworkers are also tourists of a sort, most bring cameras, whether or not these are central to research design. It is always nice to have shots of your research site for professional presentations as well as for family and friends. One researcher noted, however, that you generally want slides for professional seminars but prints for souvenirs or as small gifts to helpful locals. She thus advised bringing two

---

Ode to Ziploc Bags

The rain was coming at me sideways and even the mongrel dogs had headed for higher ground. It was three days into the trip, and although I thought it was bound to clear up soon, the sun wasn't to appear for another three days. The rain just kept falling.

I had put myself on a fairly tight schedule for data collection in Magsaysay, and there wasn't much room for downtime. Fearing a mutiny by my enumerators, I decided to keep pushing, putting my faith in the Ziplocs. I'm not sure, but I figure I must have been the only person within a thousand miles with some Ziploc bags. We kept everything in them: the completed surveys, the unfinished surveys, the camera, our dirty socks. Things we needed to keep dry went into them, and things we didn't want to leak went into them. Sometimes we double-bagged just to be sure. I kept my clipboard in one, carefully placing the bag so that I could write inside it. For three days I measured fields with rain pouring off my hat onto a Ziploc bag.

For my money, the two-gallon size is the best: plenty of room, less chance of a rip, and they'll fit on your head, functioning fairly well as a makeshift hat. I'd say take fifty, minimum. If you're going to be in the rough, don't skimp. Get the heavy-duty freezer bags. For dusty conditions, they'll keep your laptop clean. And as gifts to folks in rural areas, almost nothing seems quite as useful; keeping bugs out of the sugar is rural reality.

JERRY SHIVELY

cameras: one for slides and the other for prints. Good quality film developing can be hard to find in some countries. It pays to ask around before delivering a precious roll to an unknown outfit. Otherwise, either arrange with someone at home to process film mailed to them or store used films (in a clean, dry, cool place) until the return home. Also, remember that some film is sensitive to the x-ray equipment used in many developing country airports. Protective lead bags are low-cost, simple preventatives. Also, Kodachrome slide film is often difficult to process overseas, so Ektachrome may prove more convenient.

Equipment does not have to be big or expensive to be important. Some small-size examples, such as staplers, have already been discussed. Mechanical pencils, spare lead, Post-It notes in all sizes, and clipboards for all research assistants have repeatedly proved indispensable for one coauthor's survey work in rural Africa. Jerry Shively's testimonial to Ziploc bags (see above) demonstrates the importance of some simple items in an especially vivid way.

Transportation

You will face some transportation needs in-country. If you work in multiple or especially remote sites, you will need to pay more attention to transport issues than if you do archival work in a single city with reliable public transportation. In some areas, the timing of your research affects transportation. Monsoon season turns many non-macadam routes into impassable bogs. Plan accordingly.

It is often true that the simpler you live, the less complex things are. Thus, if you live and work in an urban area you may find public transportation a less expensive and time-consuming and more enjoyable and flexible way of moving about than a purchased or rented vehicle. Furthermore, a vehicle creates yet another tangible disparity between you and the subjects of your research. In some circumstances, this can be a serious impediment to good research, so consider such possible effects when deciding whether to acquire a vehicle.

Researchers with disabilities face special challenges in many developing country settings. Buses in most developing countries never seem to stop but just slow down a bit for passengers to enter and exit, and are invariably packed with jostling bodies. Trains and subways are not necessarily much better. So public transportation is not always an option for those with special needs. At the same time, private transport is not always superior since hand-control modifications or other adaptive mechanisms are often unavailable or might not fit the makes of vehicles available on site. More fundamentally, attitudinal barriers regarding the capabilities of disabled persons can be maddeningly ubiquitous. Researchers with disabilities need to make logistical arrangements well in advance to preempt such difficulties and to prepare for inevitable frustrations.

For researchers working in rural areas, public transport by bus, train, or "bush taxi" can consume enormous amounts of time and can subject you to truly terrifying journeys. Still, many of us delight in our tales of public transport adventure and believe all fieldworkers should experience this, if only once. Unfortunately, local bus and bush taxi systems are often inadequate for getting to and from multiple research sites, especially in remote areas. Also, the more people you need to transport, the more economical and convenient it becomes to have a vehicle of your own.

The expenses of having a vehicle include not just the purchase or rental price but maintenance costs, fuel costs, garaging and insurance. The paperwork requirements for clearing a vehicle, whether shipped from overseas or purchased locally, can also be tedious. As with computers and other research equipment, there will likely be some sort of import tax on any vehicle brought in from abroad, so budget for that. There are constant security concerns, and acquisition of a vehicle often gives the researcher unanticipated responsibilities, as we discuss in more detail below. In short, possessing a vehicle abroad entails the same hassles and conveniences—and maybe a bit more of each—as at home.

The first choice is what sort of vehicle to use. Bicycles offer not just a means of transport, but a form of exercise as well. As we discussed in Chapter 4, many fieldworkers find regular physical activity crucial to relieving stress and staying healthy. However, bicyclists may be less safe on the shoulderless roads of developing countries, especially when competing with seemingly suicidal motorized-vehicle drivers. Furthermore, poorly maintained roads can take a severe toll on all but the sturdiest mountain bikes. Few of those we consulted for this book regularly used bicycles in the field.

Motorcycles generally handle difficult road conditions better than bicycles, are often more mobile cross-country than non–four-wheel-drive cars or trucks, and are relatively economical in terms of fuel and maintenance. But, again, there are serious safety issues involved in riding in places where driving customs and laws are considerably more lax than in Europe or North America. There is also the issue of having space enough on the bike to transport necessary equipment. For these reasons, virtually all the researchers we surveyed used a car or truck if they had their own transportation.

The second choice concerns whether to buy or rent. There is no clearcut rule as to which approach is least expensive or least risky. A rental offers known but sometimes much higher costs. A good rental company also can offer emergency maintenance support and experienced drivers, which may be of real value. If you buy, vehicle resale prospects are often uncertain. Some respondents report selling their vehicles at or above the original purchase price; they were out only the cost of fuel and maintenance. On the other hand, one researcher took a hefty loss selling his used car in his agricultural site before his preharvest departure; all the locals had their money tied up in unharvested crops. In an unusually extreme case, one contributor not only lost the resale value of his four-wheel-drive vehicle when he was caught in a war zone and his truck was seized by an invading general, but he could not claim the loss from his insurer since the policy did not cover acts of war!

Buying vehicles, especially used ones, takes some skill. First, like car buying in wealthier nations, it is a bargaining sport. If you lack the stomach for such theatrics, prepare to pay a premium. And just like buying a used vehicle at home, unless you are a good mechanic yourself, bring one along to inspect the vehicle thoroughly before you commit to a purchase. A clunker can cost a fortune in maintenance. As one researcher noted, "with a premium on the time to be spent on research, hassling with a lousy car is emphatically not worth it." Other scholars about to leave the country are prime sources for serviceable vehicles and other durable equipment.

Also be forewarned that in some parts of the world (e.g., Central America) there is quite active traffic in stolen parts and vehicles. In Nairobi, there is allegedly a place where one can buy back tires stolen off one's car the night before. More seriously, there is always the danger of purchasing a car whose papers appear in order until the police pull you over. One researcher reported knowing someone who swore he repurchased his own car three times after a series of thefts and cross-border migrations!

Assuming you choose a car or truck, certain issues emerge for both purchased and rented vehicles. Do you hire a driver? The expenses involved are obvious—not just the driver's salary, but any additional expenses (lodging, meals) you might need to cover on unusually long trips. Furthermore, a driver means further loss of privacy, which may already be difficult to obtain. The advantages of a driver are freedom from the burden of driving (for those who consider driving a burden), an extra person along when difficulties inevitably arise, and perhaps better contacts for getting spare parts or fuel in areas or at times when such things are scarce. When possible, get a driver who is a skilled mechanic as well. On some fortunate occasions, a driver can offer unanticipated research benefits as well. One of the coauthors found his driver to be an unexpectedly valuable asset in building a sample frame of long-haul transporters and in securing the confidence and cooperation of trucker respondents in a study of food marketing.

Many countries have unreliable distribution systems for fuel, spare parts, and other things necessary to keep a research project going. In such places it often pays to stockpile some basic, relatively inexpensive spare parts (e.g., hoses, belts, plugs, tires) and fuel. Such a stash must be kept secure. A coauthor used a double-locked shed, under a shade tree (to help prevent an explosion when temperatures peaked) and away from his dwelling (in case the fuel blew up anyway—thankfully it did not). When fuel deliveries were interrupted for a week to ten days on three different occasions, the stockpile of fuel in forty-liter cans kept the project on schedule. It also provided an opportunity to build goodwill by refueling a truck and a few motorcycles for a local, nongovernmental organization (NGO) and agricultural extension agents.

Drivers' licenses, although a necessity, are rarely a complication for fieldwork. In the United States you can easily get an international driver's license through any American Automobile Association (AAA) office, which last for one year but are renewable. In many countries, a valid driver's license from your home jurisdiction will suffice. Just make sure it does not expire during the field research period.

Maps are essential to anyone traveling through the countryside. While maps are less readily available in stores, gas stations, and the like than in North America, bookstores and national cartographic agencies usually offer serviceable (if not always current) ones. Be warned, however, that in a few countries maps are still considered security items obtainable only through the military and with proper clearance.

Insurance, at least collision and liability coverage, is legally required in many places and a sensible thing to purchase in any case. Before anything happens, know what you need to file a claim. Most countries have reliable local insurance vendors who can provide you with a policy suited to your needs and with relatively convenient local claims procedures. There are also international policies available for purchase from home. Check with your own insurance provider or try contacting international insurance brokers. In any case, an insurer with whom you do not already have a relationship will generally require some documentation of your driving record and insurance experience; at a minimum, such paper will win a reduced premium (assuming a clean record).

Garaging a vehicle raises the same physical security issues you confront in major metropolitan areas of industrial countries. A secure parking area or a hired watchman is the best defense against robbery or vandalism. In many places it is foolish to try to save on these expenses.

Accidents happen, and in remote areas these can prove serious for even seemingly minor injuries. Airbags are nonexistent and even seatbelts are somewhat rare in vehicles obtained in developing countries. Caution is the order of the day on the road. Again, you will appreciate the value of a basic, well-stocked first-aid kit. But even in the fortunate cases where there are no injuries, you may still need to deal with property damages. This process is more or less like that at home, involving insurance companies, the police, and sometimes the court system. Still, the systems often function quite differently than you might expect based on prior home experience. Resign yourself to spending a seemingly interminable amount of time resolving the administrative and legal matters and repairing your vehicle, if necessary.

A vehicle brings with it many responsibilities. The obvious ones concern maintenance and safe driving. Not so obvious but equally important social responsibilities can emerge when you have a vehicle in areas where few people have access to such a luxury. You will commonly be solicited for rides. In some cases, these will be pedestrians-turned-hitchhikers. Follow your own judgment about this, as you would at home. One researcher had a young man jump into the flatbed of her pickup truck without her permission. He then fell and the researcher bore the responsibility for his medical costs, since the unwritten rule in that location was that "those wealthy enough to have cars should bear responsibility for the passengers, no matter who is to blame for accidents."

Several of us have found ourselves designated (without our prior agreement) as the community supply truck and ambulance. When the local mission priest or the director of the regional schools finds himself out of fuel and the nearest station is one hundred kilometers north, it is invariably the foreign researcher with a truck and fuel cans who is called on to fetch fifty liters. While the opportunity to help is almost surely welcomed, the timing of such requests-cum-demands is often inconvenient.

More seriously, health clinics in remote areas are rarely well stocked and serious illnesses or injuries usually need attention in major cities. A researcher with a vehicle can provide an invaluable service in these circumstances; the bigger the vehicle the better, since whole families often accompany an evacuating member. Of course, it is an inconvenience, consuming considerable time and fuel, and too often includes soiling your vehicle with blood, diarrhea, urine, or vomit. But whose research is more important than the health of the subjects of that study? Such events provide a dramatic opportunity to give something back to a community from which you are extracting a fair amount, to share the fruits of your privilege, to demonstrate to the community in which you are working that you sincerely care about them and their circumstances, that they are not just so many lab mice in the foreign scientists' eyes.

When serving as ambulance driver, it often pays to stick around the hospital for a bit since a foreign accent may draw more timely treatment. The role of ambulance provider can be a trying one emotionally. Sometimes you are a savior; sometimes you wind up just transporting dead bodies. One researcher commented that such serious and emotional responsibilities are "the single most difficult thing about fieldwork. It is something I can never get used to, and it is the factor that makes me feel most burnt out and in need of a break."

Research Assistants

Most overseas field researchers hire someone to assist them at some point in the research project. Assistants are sometimes hired for simple and short-term tasks. Secretarial support for projects such as questionnaire layout or data entry of completed questionnaires can be helpful. Local guides are sometimes necessary to lead you to villages drawn randomly into a survey (since such villages, after all, are inevitably not properly located on your map and may lie several kilometers' trudge through thick jungle or up a steep escarpment). Other assistants are hired for complex, multifaceted work over the duration of the project. Common examples include transcription and translation of interviews or survey enumeration.

Whether the employment is short or long term, complex or simple, and with only a few exceptions (e.g., local guides), hiring someone requires not just paying a salary or wage and benefits but also training and supervision. Carefully weigh the costs and benefits of taking on a research assistant of any sort. One contributor regretted having hired someone in the latter part of his fieldwork:

> This proved not to be worth the effort, since more time and money was spent explaining how to do what it was that I wanted . . . than actual work accomplished. Moreover, since I couldn't pay much, there was little incentive for the assistant to work very conscientiously. Based on this experience, I don't think it makes sense to have a research assistant unless there is ample money budgeted for it. Otherwise, it is simply an exercise in frustration.

If you employ research assistants, the validity of the research project hinges substantially on the quality of their work. You must screen, train, and supervise carefully and provide the appropriate incentives, both positive and negative, if you want to complete the project satisfactorily. This is an enormous, sometimes difficult, and often deeply rewarding management experience for which many academic researchers appear quite ill prepared. Many scholars identified the management of research assistants as one of the greatest challenges they faced in the field. Indeed, one person claimed that "logistical and personnel matters may take primacy over academic issues in data collection. . . . Several years' experience in the military was, quite frankly, more valuable to running a good survey than three years' doctoral training."

We cannot overemphasize the importance of the human dimensions of research. Compassion for your enumerators, mutual trust, and patience are necessary ingredients to a successful survey. Careful supervision cannot compensate for a difficult interpersonal climate on the research team. A considerable literature addresses issues of research team composition and dynamics (some of which is identified in the bibliography). We do not pretend that this chapter covers those matters thoroughly. Our objective here is to call your attention to various administrative, logistical, and human relations questions surrounding the use of field assistants.

If you think you might have use for an assistant, the first questions to ask yourself are for what function, and for how long? One researcher hired a fulltime research assistant for his one-year project, then added enumerators on an as-needed basis. When you need to conduct interviews in many different languages or when there are short bursts of intense interviewing activity punctuated by longer periods of analysis or archival research, this may be a cost-effective strategy. Think through your specific needs before setting out to find an assistant. Also, consider recruiting and training an alternate or two, especially for larger survey projects.

There is no single best method for recruiting good research assistants. Many reseachers rely on recommendations from other researchers (both local and foreign) with experience in the region, from government officials, from host university collaborators, or from nongovernmental organizations operating in the area. Some use personal contacts, established in bars, churches, hotels, or restaurants. The process relies as much on serendipity as science.

Once you have identified a pool of interested prospective research assistants, you need to screen them. Most of our respondents who hired assistants employed the usual devices: a curriculum vitae, and conversations with or letters from references. Some, especially those who fielded formal surveys, went further and gave prospective hires a test: for aptitude in filling out a sample questionnaire, for comprehension of the key concepts and terms of the research, or for the ability to think through and resolve difficult interviewing situations. Still others selected a pool of finalists for paid training, then chose assistants and alternates from that trained pool. This is a more expensive and time-consuming approach, but provides a far better chance to observe candidates' behaviors and abilities, both intellectual and interpersonal.

There are no variables that stand out as more important than others in choosing able assistants. The demands of the research design, local cultural mores, and your own skills and financial resources all considerably influence the choice of assistant(s), and in ways that are undoubtedly idiosyncratic to particular projects. Based on the research design, you may have preferences for locals or outsiders, men or women, assistants of a particular religion, or those with special language skills. For those doing formal survey work, the prospective assistant's attention to detail, handwriting, personal appearance, and basic arithmetic skills may be factors to consider as well. The assistant's general attitude, intelligence, work ethic, and sensitivity obviously matter to their likelihood of success, but such things are usually only discovered well into a research project, if at all. You inevitably act on intuition and weak indicators, and should expect to make some hiring mistakes.

Although university students and recent graduates often comprise the bulk of the applicant pool, and foreign graduate students undertaking dissertation research are often sympathetic to this group, several researchers were disappointed by the reliability and work ethic of university student assistants. The basic issue appears to be that students often have insufficient time for the intense work schedules of most overseas field research projects, and may not have the maturity necessary to resolve difficult situations. Moreover, in many circumstances university students are outsiders in the communities under investigation—in class, ethnic, and regional terms—and are perceived as such, sometimes degrading their usefulness to the researcher. That said, the pace of work overseas generally differs from that to which workaholic academics in North American and European universities are accustomed. This can be frustrating but can also provide unexpected insights on the cultural setting and the myriad demands on the residents of your research site. Several scholars remarked that they found married adults to be the most reliable assistants: mature, hardworking, disciplined, but sensitive. Others favored local secondary-school graduates. Familiarity with local customs and dialects is indispensable. Locals often bring with them useful contacts, but sometimes they also carry troublesome relationship histories. There are no clear demographic rules of thumb about who makes a good research assistant, only behavioral ones: you need someone honest, pleasant, patient, responsible, and reasonably intelligent.

Several researchers drew up written contracts laying out the terms of compensation, supervision, conditions of termination by either party, and the period of employment. The researcher and assistant both signed the contract. While such documents might seem rather stiff and formal, they are often necessary to ensure that all parties have a clear understanding of everyone's rights and responsibilities. Indeed, a couple of respondents who struck more informal agreements with assistants came to wish they had formalized the terms of employment.

Incentives matter. One researcher notes wryly that

> the very structure of doing survey work is such that enumerators have exactly the opposite incentives as the researcher has.

The researcher wants to get the job done quickly; the enumerators want it to last as long as possible. The researcher wants good, high-quality data, even if it takes extra effort to get it. The enumerator isn't going to be around to help with data entry, let alone analysis, so has fewer cares about the quality of the data. Nothing demoralizes everybody like having tension between a researcher and his or her enumerators, but they inevitably arise in the course of doing a survey.

In other words, you must take incentives into account explicitly.

The most obvious incentive is the assistant's salary or wage. Several scholars supplemented a fixed regular (monthly, weekly, or daily) stipend with performance bonuses to provide extra incentives for careful work and completion of the project. In addition to individual bonuses based on the researcher's subjective assessment of the quality of an assistant's work, at least one researcher also offered team bonuses for finishing project modules (e.g., the enumeration of a village) on schedule. Another offered a per diem for extended periods spent in the field, calculated to be slightly more than an enumerator's necessary expenses and, thus, helped induce teams to spend time in survey sites rather than at home in the regional capital. Similarly, several used graduated pay scales, wherein the fixed regular stipend increased over time as the assistant gained experience, presumably becoming more productive and indispensable to the project. This likewise provided inducements to sustained careful work by the assistants.

Assistants hired for longer periods of time or for hazardous work should be provided explicit benefits. Just as you need and deserve breaks from the grind of fieldwork, so do assistants. Build some vacation into longer contracts. You may want to build in sick days as well, and plan contingencies for extended illness. Do you pay an assistant full rate, a reduced rate, or not at all when she falls ill or is injured due to no fault of hers or the researcher's? It is hard to know the right thing to do, but you should think through such scenarios and discuss them with your assistant(s). A number of researchers provided health insurance, either through a third-party insurer or on their own, by paying assistants' medical expenses during the project, especially for work-related illness or injury.

Given the enormous importance of good research assistance to most fieldwork projects, it is difficult to compensate good enumerators adequately. While researchers often pay great attention to the monetary benefits offered, bear in mind the nonmonetary benefits as well. In many locales, there exists a broader cultural understanding of contractual relations, especially in labor relations, that encompasses symbols of appreciation and loyalty, not just a paycheck or western-style benefits. Pride in the project, respectful treatment by one's colleagues, and an opportunity to learn more about a foreign land or language can go a long way toward compensating assistants for hard work on a project of finite duration. Several researchers threw small, regular parties for the research team or paid for rounds of chilled soft drinks in the middle of hot afternoons. Some invested time in writing a formal letter of recommendation that assistants could subsequently use to help gain further work, and some have gone one step further, helping find postproject employment or academic opportunities for their assistants. One researcher set aside a bit of research money to enroll her assistants in a computer training class to make them more employable after the project ended.

Research assistants are partners, if sometimes (but not always) junior ones, in the research effort. You can never go wrong giving them due acknowledgment in scholarly books and articles. Some scholars have included assistants as coauthors, and several have sent copies of their final published products back to assistants as a memento of the experience (and a useful tool in landing future research assistantships).

If the research project will take assistants away from their homes, it is your obligation to ensure all team members are adequately housed and fed. Enumerator teams that migrate from village to village will generally need basic supplies such as sleeping mats, a couple of pots, candles, matches, a first-aid kit (including malaria prophylaxis, if needed), a flashlight, and batteries. One of the coauthors used a couple of hundred dollars of grant money to purchase such field equipment, then auctioned all of it off at an end-of-project party, redistributing the proceeds as bonuses to those assistants who completed the project.

Incentives are not the only, or even the major, factor in research assistant performance. Training assistants in an unfamiliar setting and, often, in an unfamiliar language can be a logistical and pedagogical nightmare. It is nonetheless essential to any formal survey work and desirable for many informal research methods as well. Not only does a training period permit you to communicate research objectives and the detail of research methods clearly and repeatedly to your assistants, it also helps foster camaraderie among a team that will soon work intensively together. This makes the research experience more fruitful and more enjoyable. If you need hired assistance, it is generally wise to invest the time and resources necessary to train assistants properly before launching into the body of the research project. Aili Tripp emphasizes below the need for mutual input into field research.

In the ideal, you train assistants to substitute for the lead researcher, so that if you become incapacitated or communications or transport difficulties separate the team, the project can continue apace without any serious degradation in performance. Nonetheless,

---

Building Partnership

In working with research assistants, I have found it important to explain the project objectives (I give them my proposal), methods, and what my expectations are of them as assistants. But I also try to find out about their expectations and solicit their advice on the research project, especially from assistants who have done research before. Since I know I am going to rely heavily on them, I think of them as partners, not simply employees. In the course of the research, I try to create an atmosphere of mutual learning and shared experiences between myself and my assistant(s) and also among them if there is more than one assistant. I have always selected key assistants who were geniunely interested in my research topic and have rarely, if ever, been disappointed. Their work and enthusiasm has often gone beyond the call of duty, and I have been able to benefit from their invaluable insights.

I also try to think of ways in which the research and their contact with me can benefit them beyond simply being a source of income. Much depends on the goals and interests of the individual. One assistant was able to use our findings to write her M.A. thesis and then went on to pursue a Ph.D. Another coauthored a paper with me and participated in symposia and roundtables I organized in North America. I did what I could to assist most of them in continuing their education and obtaining further employment.

AILI TRIPP

this ideal is seldom even closely approximated. Among our respondents, assistant training ranged from none at all (which led to a disaster) to a formal multiweek session of classroom workshops and field testing. Several of us have borrowed a classroom and spent time reviewing interviewing techniques, questionnaire design, coding, variable definitions, translations, the paper trail for questionnaires, and administrative issues regarding pay, transport, lodging, and more. Some researchers conduct the training themselves; others hire locals in whom they have great confidence to direct the training.

Supervision is also crucial if you hope to avoid shirking and sloppiness on the part of enumerators. By no means do we wish to encourage distrust of your assistants. Nevertheless, you must recognize that, as pointed out earlier, enumerators sometimes have incentives to cut corners, whether due to laziness, a desire to impress or support the researcher, or some other factor. Regular (ideally, daily) spot-checking, built-in validity checks, and discussions with respondents about the interviews can be valuable diagnostic tools in establishing whether assistants are following the research design properly. When possible, hold small group meetings in the evening to review the day's data and interviewing experiences while fresh in everyone's mind. This can serve as a valuable exercise in data quality control.

If you are prepared to hire assistants, you must also be prepared to fire them, unpleasant as it is. Tolerance of sloppiness can destroy the entire research project. Several researchers reported having to fire assistants, and were often surprised that the dismissals "did not result in any tension in the study village[s]" nor in the team of assistants.

Research assistants often become longer-term collaborators and lifelong friends. Many researchers echoed one person's remark, "I don't know how I would have survived my time in Uganda if I had not been friends with my assistants as well. We socialized together and enjoyed each other's company." Nonetheless, be cautious about mixing friendship with work. The power relationship between the researcher and the assistant is often more complex than it first appears. As locals with advantages of language, contacts, and familiarity with local customs and institutions, assistants can enjoy certain claims and status not possessed by the foreign researcher. The powers of race, wealth, being a guest, and, sometimes, age, nonetheless accrue to the fieldworker. Negotiation of these relationships ranges from congenial and cooperative to competitive to outright conflictive, and cannot be fully anticipated. Pay attention to these relationships.

Several scholars had nightmarish experiences with relationships. One researcher discovered her assistant was in a complicated love triangle involving a member of the household in which she was living. She let the assistant go amid ill-will and embarrassment. Another researcher, who took her assistant in as a housemate (and paid for all the living expenses), encountered conflicts:

> My problem was that I had a hard time distinguishing between my roles as employer and friend. I took my job so personally that I found it impossible to work and live with my assistant when we were not getting along. It made it easy for her to make what I felt were unreasonable demands on me, for I just wanted to avoid a big confrontation that would bring my work to a halt. Eventually it became too difficult for us to work together. She was miserable, and had developed health problems as a reaction to her environment. I gave her some money and sent her away. I think we both realized that it wasn't a good idea for us to work together any longer, though I felt really guilty for taking her job away, knowing that jobs are so difficult to find.

As is the case with other logistical and administrative matters surrounding field research, the use of research assistants demands prior planning, patience, and flexibility. The joys and trials of your experience, sometimes even the success or failure of the entire venture, often turn on your handling issues that may seem ancillary to the research project. There are no tried and true recipes for identifying and resolving the myriad logistical challenges of fieldwork. Still, we hope this chapter has been of help in raising important questions, offering useful advice, relaying amusing and instructive experiences, or simply providing an assurance that most social scientists endure frustration and embarrassment as a regular—and character-building—part of the experience of fieldwork.

6

The Challenges of the Field

Many texts on research methods treat technical issues and, as a consequence, are not always useful to a researcher in the field when unpredictable situations crop up, as they often do. You undoubtedly will find yourself confronted with circumstances for which orthodox methods learned from texts and graduate courses are ill suited. First-rate scholarship advances, but the keys to success are likely to be the creativity, perseverance, and training of the researcher.

Not all improvisation is well advised or effective, however. In this chapter, we discuss some issues common to many research projects but not usually addressed in methods texts. We do not provide cookbook solutions—many of the experiences we relate are idiosyncratic. We seek only to stimulate thought about how creative solutions can be found to unexpected obstacles. In particular, we address some of the not-so-obvious issues involved in choosing informants, cross-checking data, facing sensitive research topics, and, finally, finding ways to maintain credibility in the field. Throughout this discussion we consider more informal aspects of research methods, since most researchers reported that "textbook" methods were not always helpful given the unpredictable nature of fieldwork.

Choosing and Cultivating Informants

When you go into the field, one of the first things you have to figure out is who to talk to or who to survey. Since you learn through the people with whom you come into contact, care must be taken in choosing and cultivating informants. That said, there is no single recipe for such selection and no generalizable advice about the best ways to make informants feel comfortable with the researcher. Field-workers we surveyed used an extremely wide array of methods to come up with interesting and useful information about their research topics. For example, when doing research focused on political and economic elites, you can usually figure out the important people to interview by reading old newspapers and by going to research institutes to find people who may be familiar with your topic of interest. In contrast, if you are working in a rural area, you will need to quickly locate yourself within informal social networks to discover who are the most appropriate informants.

Experienced researchers uniformly emphasize the need to establish solid informal relationships with informants. In some cases this will be much more important than in others. Generally speaking, the anthropologist will need to establish longer term personal relationships than might a political scientist. Without informal, nonprofessional contact with informants, the research process is often quite frustrating.

One anthropologist illustrates the importance of informal contact in describing her method of choosing informants and her treatment of these informants after they had been selected (see below).

This account emphasizes the importance of considering what will encourage informants to cooperate. The issue of remunerating respondents has been long contested in the research methods literature, and we do not include the above example as an endorsement of respondent compensation. Instead, the point is this: Although you might be able to identify the best possible informants through diligent research, unless you earn their trust and motivate their participation, you probably will not get very far and your understanding of local circumstances will be limited.

You should be careful not to give the appearance of "using" informants. This is a tricky business when you think realistically about the research process; after all, most researchers are, in fact, using informants. You will not get the information sought without their cooperation. We simply point out that you should make sure that the process is not a one-way street. We will have more to say about the ways in which you can give something back to informants in subsequent chapters.

That said, keep in mind that some informants will not care whether they receive anything back. Public figures, such as government officials, political figures, prominent business people, sometimes even academic "stars," often do not expect or want anything from the researcher. As a consequence, some scholars caution against having high expectations of VIPs. As one political scientist put it, "I discovered quickly that I wasn't going to get much more than the official public statement out of even the ones I had imagined would be relaxed and 'honest.'" Most field researchers have to do quite a bit of digging to find informants who will give useful information and who will not worry about compromising their image.

If you use more formal sampling techniques, you have a different set of worries. Although often concerned with speaking to or surveying individuals, you may not care who these individuals are. Never-

Personal Relationships and the Research Process

One of the objectives of my study was to find out basic household economic information to develop a picture of how returned refugees achieved or failed to achieve self-sufficiency, and to figure out how self-sufficiency was defined. I instinctively felt in the first year of research that I didn't know the people well enough to ask them to participate in an economic survey of this nature. Tigrayans are very secretive about their income, and go to great lengths to hide their wealth from each other (even from other family members) and especially from the local government. I needed to convince people that I didn't work for the government, or the United Nations, and that if I promised to protect their confidentiality, I could be trusted.

To gain the confidence of my respondents, I wrote a one-page letter of consent that I translated into Tigrinya. I read it out loud to each potential respondent household and had the head sign or put his or her thumbprint on it. This letter assured respondents that none of the information they gave me would be used in such a way that they could be identified by it. It said that I would not tell the local government or other community members what kind of information they were providing me with. If they decided at any

theless, do not assume that random sampling techniques make the research process any easier. As Steve Boucher points out (pp. 94–95), the struggle to define the sampling frame from which to draw respondents at random can be a serious problem in itself.

If any single lesson can be drawn from this and other experiences, it is that the researcher must be creative and persistent in discovering appropriate informants. Many leads will go nowhere, and adjustments will be necessary during the research process.

We also call attention to Boucher's precise definition of the unit of analysis in his work in Mozambique. Many empirical social scientists fail to define precisely their unit(s) of analysis at an early stage and so cast about in an uncoordinated grab at data that ultimately prove difficult, if not impossible, to integrate. This problem often results from the disjuncture common between units of analysis in the

time that they did not want to participate, or if they decided at some point that they had given information that they wanted to retract, they were free to do so. The letter also stated that they would not derive any direct benefit from participating in the study while it was being conducted. The survey was quite a commitment of time, however, requiring half-hour interviews every day for four months, so I included the promise that at the end of the study I would give them their choice of a goat or a sheep as payment. My primary goal in presenting this letter was to cover myself by ensuring that I had the proper consent required by the Committee for the Protection of Human Subjects at the University of Wisconsin, but it was also meant to make them feel that even though they had signed a letter, they had not forfeited their control over participation in the study. No one took advantage of the opportunity to withdraw from the study, but I think that knowing that that option was there and that their confidentiality was guaranteed encouraged respondents to be more honest than they might otherwise have been. When I eventually gave the payment, most respondents said that they had participated out of friendship to me, and that reward was unnecessary, though appreciated.

LAURA HAMMOND

Finding the Appropriate Sampling Frame

In three of my fieldwork experiences I drew formal, random samples. This is a critical stage of research and a stage for which there is usually no formal training. One suggestion, perhaps obvious but nonetheless important, is to define very clearly the unit of analysis. For example, in Mozambique we were interested in analyzing how price liberalization was affecting the dynamism of land markets and the access of low-wealth households to agricultural land. Our principle unit of analysis was the agricultural plot. We needed to find as comprehensive a list as possible of all individual plots in our specific regions. This was perhaps the most time-consuming component of the entire research project. We first needed a random sample of all titled plots. While this was to have been relatively straightforward, in practice, it was quite a mess. When I was initially informed that any formal urban or agricultural land must be listed in the Office of Land Registry, I immediately headed there. There I was told that almost all "titled" plots were operating without formal title since the process of officializing the title was so time-consuming and expensive that virtually nobody took this last formal step. At that point I thought that the project was finished since our theory regarding the impact of title on land prices had no application in Maputo. Upon further conversation with farmers, however, I became confused because many of those with loans told me that they had used their "formal" land title as collateral. From there I headed to one of the bank branches to find out what is regarded as sufficiently "formal" collateral. One bank manager informed me that a document registered in Maputo's municipality was sufficient. Since the plots we were analyzing were in peri-urban zones, the land titling agency was a branch of the offices of the municipality.

After tracking down the functionary responsible for the filing of peri-urban titles, I learned that his office was the last stop in the titling process before the Office of Land Registry. He showed me a very detailed map of all the parcels in the areas we were working in and suggested it would be no problem to randomly choose two hundred of the five hundred titled parcels, since each parcel was represented by an index card, which were stacked in a corner of his desk.

At this point I was very excited since it seemed that sample selection would be quite easy, but the excitement lasted only until he said, "There's only one little problem." The problem was that in 1991 one of the regions we were working in had been officially transferred to another municipality's jurisdiction. I asked why this was a problem, since the index cards for that area should be in the other municipality's office. The problem, he said, was that when the relocation occurred, a truck came to his office into which some men loaded all documentation related to the areas to be reassigned. "Why is this a problem?" I asked. Apparently, somewhere between the two municipal offices, the truck got lost and never showed up. Having come this far, I was not about to give up. So I tracked down the official in charge of municipal vehicles to see if he had any suggestions. Unfortunately, that job had been contracted to the military. After several more days I located a military official who had been involved in the incident. After spending some time convincing the official that I really wasn't interested in stealing state secrets, but only in finding lost land titles, he escorted me to several warehouses where low priority documents were stored and said that maybe he remembered something about some municipal documents being dumped here. After sifting through ceiling-high piles of documents, I found the missing index cards and was able to draw the sample.

STEVE BOUCHER

theory that informs one's work (e.g., association, firm, household, party, state) and the individual unit of inquiry operationalized in most primary data collection. You need to be attentive to, and sometimes creative about, units of analysis in fieldwork.

Cross-Checking Data

No matter the method used, you will almost always face a dilemma: How do you know that the information being accumulated is accurate? How do you know that informants are honest? Such questions do not necessarily arise from a suspicion that informants lack integrity. You can imagine, in fact, a wide variety of reasons why informants might fudge their answers or misunderstand the question(s) asked. While deception may at times be motivated by a self-interested concern for wealth or reputation, informants might equally fear the political, social, or economic consequences of their words, or they might be telling you what they think you want to hear.

There are various ways to handle these problems. You might enlarge your sample, although this will not help much if the research techniques themselves are flawed. A common and effective way is, as one researcher put it, "the time-honored technique of triangulation—in other words, using a number of different methods and sources to obtain the same information—thereby verifying the veracity—or not—of the information." This same researcher noted that an effective way of finding out if you have got the facts right is to share findings with "particularly knowledgeable individuals (e.g., key informants)." An important way to be reasonably sure of getting the right information is through overlapping methods. A mix of qualitative and quantitative methods often provides an effective way to ensure that conclusions bear a fair relationship to reality. Sitting in on the interviews conducted by assistants helps to validate the information assistants reported.

If you have enough time in the field, it may be possible to cross-check data using different methods and repeating your work with a new twist. One scholar discovered the importance of being able to make adjustments in the middle of the research experience, which almost always makes for a more valuable end product:

> I ran a two-round survey, and after the first round of the survey
> it was clear that the initial case studies had not covered all the
> territory they should have, so we carried out several more in be-

tween rounds of the survey. At this point, the case studies were less exploratory and more focused on particular topics. After the second round of the survey, we conducted a number of focus group discussions—both with survey respondents and with groups in areas where we had not done any survey work. These turned out to be invaluable, not so much in the sense of providing new data, but in correcting some misinterpretations of case study and survey data, and in offering answers to questions that arose out of survey data.

Broaching Sensitive Subjects

In the course of fieldwork, many researchers find—if they were not already aware—that the information that they are collecting is very sensitive. The information might be sensitive because it concerns subjects people feel uncomfortable talking about (e.g., religious rites, sexuality) or because disclosure could harm the informant (e.g., disclosure of illegal activities or taxable wealth). Thinking through the ethics and the research practices associated with protecting your informants is mandatory if you are dealing with politically or socially sensitive issues. We strongly advise you to establish your own guidelines before going to the field.

You may confront unexpected sensitivity dilemmas. Keep in mind that what an outsider might consider innocuous or mundane may prove extremely sensitive in a particular research context. Aside from possibly causing harm by action or inaction (more on this below), the unexpected sensitivity of certain issues can lead to inaccurate data. One scholar pointed out how this problem of unexpected sensitivity made data collection difficult:

> It was fascinating for me to see how subjects that seemed so neutral to the outsider are in fact quite sensitive to certain informants. . . . For example, in asking about food expenditures and intakes, we found two sorts of biases: on the one hand, if informants thought that we were somehow there to "judge" their eating habits, they would tend to exaggerate the data to make it seem as if they were consuming all the things that are supposed to be good for you (meat, vegetables, eggs). On the other hand, if they thought we were there for a handout, they would underreport.

It is important to clarify your data collection objectives and the ultimate disposition of the data with all respondents before surveying begins. Holding community meetings and hiring enumerators knowledgeable about local conditions and practices can help to accomplish this.

The accuracy of the data can also be affected by who is asking the questions of informants, or even just who is present at an interview. Not only is the outside researcher's race, nationality, gender, and class likely to generate certain assumptions on the part of informants, but local enumerators can affect informants' responses to questions. For example, one of the coauthors found he could not use African enumerators to interview Asian merchants—indeed, the Africans could not even be present during interviews with these respondents—because racial tensions induced blatant misreporting of observable data. Conversely, the researcher had to stay away from some interviews with respondents in areas with particularly painful memories of colonial violence because his race adversely influenced respondents' forthrightness. These unanticipated circumstances necessitated some creative juggling of surveying schedules and teams.

Beyond the dynamics of researcher/respondent interaction, sometimes the political context can dramatically affect the process of interview and data collection. As a consequence, you must be careful to protect your safety as well as that of your informants. One contributor cautioned that "political situations can evolve very rapidly; what seems fine one year might be very dangerous just a few years later." Particularly in authoritarian regimes, people can and do get killed because of the information they possess, and since the entire research process involves obtaining information, letting the wrong people know when you obtained information can be fatal. We emphasize that this is important not only in published research results but during the research process itself, when you may well have conversations with individuals who can harm your informants. Michael Sullivan, who did his work in China, explains how creativity can be employed in sensitive situations (see opposite).

The Chinese case is atypical in the lengths to which you must go to protect informants and yourself. More often than not, you can manipulate the research topic to make it sound less threatening. One scholar who worked in Central America at the end of the Reagan/ Bush period noted that "everything was sensitive. It was obvious that

---

Creatively Broaching Sensitive Subjects

My research confronted the problem of broaching sensitive subject matters. I gained the confidence of interviewees through connections with colleagues and friends of theirs. . . . Most interviewees were relatively open to my inquiries, except when it came to politically sensitive subjects. I found that interviewees tended to share their personal thoughts when they were alone with me. Even so, individuals associated with government and party organizations tended to be less forthcoming in their information even if we met privately and in a safe location.

When I met with one interviewee, I found out that he was under semi-house arrest *after* I entered his home. Since he clearly informed me that his house was bugged, we talked about politically sensitive topics with references to Western political philosophy and imperial Chinese history. The Ming emperor became a hidden way to talk about paramount leader Deng Xiaoping. We had dinner together at a local restaurant. Four security personnel followed us and sat at a table next to us. Rather than talking about democracy in China, he discussed Hegel as a way to criticize Marxism-Leninism and the Chinese Communist Party.

MICHAEL SULLIVAN

---

people wouldn't talk to me if they thought I was interested in political issues. I tried to convey the attitude that I was interested in economic policy from a technocratic perspective and that I wanted to talk to them about it technocrat to technocrat. This really worked." Obviously, you must be careful that such manipulation does not misrepresent your work, as it might lead to enormous personal and professional complications during or after the fieldwork. Nonetheless, you can usually do some "honest" manipulation of your topic to avoid unnecessary suspicion and noncooperation from informants.

On occasion, you will have to change research topics as a consequence of the sensitivity of the issues being investigated. One scholar recounted, "Early on in my time in Malaysia, I received advice from many sources that it would be difficult and risky to do research on indigenous peoples' movements in East Malaysia. I was advised that I would have to carefully camouflage my real interests" to receive research clearance, and that even if such clearance were obtained, the actual research process would be exceedingly difficult. "All of this convinced me that my original plans would not be feasible without extensive and risky subterfuge on my part." In the end, changing topics to something safer may be the best choice, and most seasoned researchers would agree that it is wise to maintain a flexible research agenda.

Working with Tape Recorders

If your research methodology requires interviewing informants—and the subject matter involves sensitive issues—you will inevitably confront a crucial question: to tape record or not to tape record interviews? There is no consensus among experienced researchers beyond the simple rule that one should never tape without the permission of the interviewee. Because of this fundamental disagreement, we simply present the pros and cons of taping and some of the important issues to consider.

Those who favor taping interviews point out that taping offers an accurate record of the interview itself, and it relieves the researcher of the burden of taking notes during the interview. The latter is a particular advantage if note-taking leads you to lose the train of the conversation or eye contact with the interviewee. Especially when interviewing in a foreign language, taping can be very valuable. Having to interrupt the flow of the interview to ask for clarification about a word or phrase can seriously impede the interview. If there is a taped record of the interview, you can figure out what was said after the interview is over. Moreover, you might realize some of the subtleties of what was said when listening to the interview a second or third time. Keep in mind, however, that taping usually requires transcription (and perhaps translation) of tapes while in the field, since, as one contributor noted, "if you let a large number of interviews pile up on tape, the temptation will be too great to simply skip the tedium of getting the data into a usable form."

The case against taping can be made simply: It may introduce substantial bias in the interview process. Respondents will be less likely to answer questions honestly if they know there is a permanent record of what they are saying, and thus may tend to be evasive, speak only in generalities, and avoid providing much useful information. The reliability of this assertion depends on the topic under discussion, the demeanor and formal position of the interviewee, and the level of trust. Hopefully, you will be able to sense whether taping will inhibit the informant's responses when asking for permission to record the interview or doing the interview itself. If during the taping you sense reticence on the part of the informant, simply ask, "Would you prefer that I turn off the tape recorder?" This might elicit important information and will signal to the interviewee your sensitivity.

If you do not tape the interview, however, you will run into the problem of how to have an accurate record of it. Some prefer taking notes during the interview, which can lead to the problems mentioned above. Others prefer to put off taking notes until after the interview is over. A colleague noted that she "did only very discrete note-taking and then immediately ran to the bathroom to jot down the rest." Others prefer to have a tape recorder with them even when they do not tape the interview, because they can quickly recount the dialogue into a tape recorder immediately after the interview. Either of these techniques requires substantial short-term memory, a trait with which not all of us are blessed.

Finally, we call attention to an important, often overlooked semantic distinction, which can have enormous consequences. Many researchers conflate "confidentiality" with "anonymity" when discussing their approach to sensitive issues. Telling an informant that something is confidential means that the *researcher will not use it* in reporting research results; the information is purely for the researcher's private edification. By contrast, the promise of anonymity simply implies that *the source will not be identified,* but that the information can be used. You must exercise care when using anonymous sources, even where the provider of information has given permission to use his or her words, if not the individual's name. "Insiders" will often be able to identify the source, which could endanger that individual. On a related note, one researcher said that "even in one's acknowledgments, one must be careful not to implicate people simply through their association with a foreign researcher." Once again, think through these ethical issues before going to the field. Most major research universities have human subjects research committees, which can provide you with established protocols regarding anonymity and confidentiality.

Handling Unexpected Challenges
to the Researcher's Credibility

We—Treasure, Futhi, and I—set out for the peri-urban community where three of the young women we'd screened at the mother-child clinic lived. The three of them fit our parameters in terms of age, size, and age of child, and had said they were interested. The first was a success. In looking for the second woman, we ran into a woman who told us that the woman we sought was not there. Our interaction was complicated and oddly hostile. I wanted to locate the correct woman or leave a message for her. Treasure wanted to explain the study to this woman, and Futhi was in a perplexingly aggressive and flippant mood. After a few minutes we left.

We crested the road leading out of this valley and stopped in the local shop for Cokes before returning to our car. Strolling along sipping our drinks, we encountered a taxi driver and a widow from the houses of the community. They told us that we had caused quite a stir. Folks were saying that we were baby-thieves like those described in the papers.

The driver seemed to think the situation was partially funny. The widow was extremely serious. I wanted to return immediately to the community and straighten the mess out but Treasure counseled waiting and Futhi joked with the taxi driver in a way that could certainly have inflamed the situation. We then allowed the two strangers to inspect our car while we appeared to be otherwise occupied. They seemed satisfied that we had no babies on us but stalked around like angry lions and took down the license number. I knew that this was not just going to blow over.

I dropped Treasure off at home and found Zenele in her cool office building and asked her advice. She said to talk to Daniel; he was at home. I buzzed USIS, where they helped me make an appointment to be interviewed on the Women's Page of the *Times* of Swaziland to get my name and face and nonthreatening activities out there before [more trouble started]. I got John Hanson at the U.S. Embassy to write a letter on fancy letterhead that stated very clearly that I was cool.

At home Daniel heard me out and agreed to return to the community with me to clear things up. We took my car and drove straight to the area and parked in the same place. Daniel ran into an acquaintance, the butcher. He advised us that the head man, whom I had consulted days earlier, was not around and suggested we speak with a much-respected retired schoolteacher.

We found the teacher, and she advised us to return to the original homestead with her granddaughter. At the homestead people began to gather. Daniel, the original woman, and the teacher's husband moved off to talk together. The rest of us formed a loose circle. A nice young guy in a Bahai tee-shirt was conversationally relocated as my occasional translator and defender. But he was teased about being my husband and "had to leave" shortly thereafter. I could hear that Daniel was facing tough opposition. The young woman said she was convinced Futhi, Treasure, and I were the people from an earlier newspaper story about people out to steal children. I was confronted by a group that was occasionally raucous and obstreperous. It became clear that this was half deadly earnest and half entertainment. One woman, who was breastfeeding a one-and-a-half-year-old on demand, went from shrieking at me that I'd come to steal children, slit their throats, and use their body parts for some unspeakably evil purpose to dancing over to me and suggesting that we trade skirts.

The interaction was mainly in siSwati but sometimes the questions came to me in English. Always, the really outraged tones and graphic accusations were directed to me in alternating phrases—first siSwati, then English. The group was trying to make me be evil, to invest me with dangerousness and despicability. It was a struggle of images. I tried to assert my own sense of myself as a guileless foreign researcher. Daniel tried to assert [himself as] a . . . slightly aggrandized medical specialist. The process of negotiating my identity rose and fell in intensity but the theme of fierce and offended mothers confronting me was consistent.

Gradually the punctuations in the interaction died down. Daniel and I, together now, continued to insist that I was innocuous and only interested in women's nutrition and work. Daniel twisted my study topic around a bit and told people that I would arrange a time with the head man's wife and come teach about pregnant women's health. The remaining people agreed that that was a good way to end things and the group dispersed.

CAROLYN BEHRMAN

Maintaining Credibility in the Field

The concept of academic research is a confusing one for many people (including loved ones, in many cases). Thus, field researchers often struggle with the process of self-definition. This will necessarily change depending on context. You will probably explain your project quite differently to a government bureaucrat than to a landless peasant. Whatever the audience, you need to maintain credibility in the eyes of those in the field site.

The beginning of the research period is often crucial in setting the appropriate tone. One practice that can help establish credibility is to make it clear to respondents and local communities that you will share research results with those who provide the raw data. A sociologist made a strong case for giving something back:

> For both ethical and methodological reasons, research feedback is absolutely imperative. I don't know how many people sighed and agreed to be interviewed but told me they were sure I would just interview them and then run back to [the national university] and never be seen or heard from again. We made a commitment to present our findings to a village meeting in each one of the enumeration areas—a meeting that not only provoked a lot of good discussion and insight, but also provided a forum to talk about the topic of research in terms of what it meant in the community.

By sharing results with local communities, you create appropriate conditions for an ongoing relationship with those in the research site. You may also help generate good will toward other researchers who follow in your wake. Perhaps you will similarly benefit from the good conduct of those who preceded you.

When dealing with an issue that may be considered a development project, expect that many in the research site will assume that you are going to bring money into the local community. This can be a particularly difficult problem to confront, since locals often will not believe protestations that a (relatively) independent researcher cannot bring in money or projects. After all, they often have good reason not to believe what foreigners tell them. The best approach is to make it very clear at the beginning of the research period what you will and will not do for respondents or the community in general. Do not promise anything that you cannot deliver. When you sense ambiguity about how people see your intentions, clarify them.

Also be prepared for the occasional unexpected challenges to your credibility. Although some measures can be taken to avoid such challenges, not everything can be foreseen. As the excerpts from Carolyn Behrman's journal make abundantly clear, wild and unexpected things happen to the foreign researcher that can threaten the entire project. The individuals mentioned in the story were either research assistants or local friends.

Recognize the limitations of your power to change the situation when incidents occur. Behrman reported that one of the local newspapers subsequently ran a story that was favorable to her, while another paper insinuated that she was indeed a baby-snatcher. She said that other researchers "expressed both amusement and discomfort with the apparent random and uncontrollable nature of the incident." The lesson of this story is rather simple: You cannot predict everything that will happen. Hopefully, you will think quickly on your feet when confronted by situations that can undermine credibility. Having local allies available and willing to intercede if necessary proves indispensable to field research efforts more frequently than is commonly acknowledged.

The research process is clearly fraught with uncontrollable situations. We hope, however, that by thinking through—especially *before* the fieldwork begins—the ethics of your conduct in the field, the potential pitfalls of research, and the typical ways in which fieldwork reality deviates from plans, your fieldwork will be both more productive and enjoyable.

7

Knowing When to Go Home

Like most of the decisions discussed in this volume, there is no universally applicable rule governing the difficult choice of when to pack up and head home. Some fieldworkers have their choices made for them. For one person, kidney failure forced medical evacuation. One contributor, caught unexpectedly in a war zone, recounted, "When I woke to the sound of MIG fighter jets overhead, incoming artillery shells and machine gun fire outside the door, I knew it was time to leave!" Only slightly less dramatic, when you run out of money and are directed by authorities to leave the country (or else!), or when your partner (or for graduate students, adviser) says come home NOW, it is almost surely time to pack up.

Most researchers, however, are not forced to leave the field so abruptly, and many retain considerable discretion over this choice. At some point you have to decide that the data and materials already collected will suffice. Often this realization occurs when you begin hearing (and believing) the same answers over and over again. To be sure, some do not reach such a saturation point for quite a long time. Typically, researchers think that they never have enough information, when in fact it is more often the case that they return with more than they could ever use in a single project. Given that most research projects are more ambitious than feasible, in this chapter we consider questions of planning the last months in the field, judging what is absolutely necessary for your project, and getting body and data home again safely.

Narrowing the Topic

If a clear focus in your field research design does not always pay off in the initial stages of finding funding or beginning fieldwork, it invariably does in the terminal period of the project. Good predeparture preparations and the exercise of discipline in the field to stick to the project rather than dash off on alluring tangents, as so many of us do, help immeasurably in getting your research wrapped up successfully and in a timely manner. We are not saying that you must stick with the original research design to the last. Many scholars consulted for this book wisely and successfully changed tack once in the field. But a good sense of the broader literature into which you are trying to fit your research, and of the data and methods necessary to pursue a given issue effectively, substantially improve your prospects for actually getting the right data, in the right ways, and in getting back home relatively quickly to pull it all together.

Several well-prepared researchers recognized quite early during their field research that their original proposals were largely irrelevant. The scholarly literature may be dated, and the information available outside the research site sometimes paints a very different picture of conditions than what you will find on the inside. Again, this makes a good case for preparatory research trips, but even these are no guarantee that your research design will prove implementable or sensible when the time comes to launch the project. One researcher suggested

> it should be anticipated that you will change or narrow the scope of your research topic while in the field—and you should be flexible enough to do this without unnecessary anguish. We cannot help but write inappropriate research proposals or outlines from thousands of miles away (unless we have been there before—another reason for a preparatory trip to the field). For some people, a lack of time is likely to be the greatest problem presented by such changes in the field. . . . In general, I think that narrowing the topic as much as possible is essential.

Another political scientist concurred in the absolute necessity of a clearly defined, manageable topic, but cautioned against assuming that you will need to change topics or research design; you run the real risk of perhaps too hastily jettisoning a valid plan on which you worked diligently for some time.

Your original research proposal, revised for changes made in the field, provides an excellent touchstone for narrowing your topic, especially in judiciously choosing how to allocate increasingly scarce resources (not the least of which is time) in the waning weeks of fieldwork. Chapter outlines of the book or dissertation on which you are working can serve a similar end, enabling you to ask yourself, "Can I answer each of the questions raised in this outline?" and "Can I test each of the hypotheses stated?" Direct your final efforts toward those areas that cause you to answer "no" to either of these questions.

Many respondents report having been forced to limit the amount of information they collected because they simply did not have as much time to collect, organize, and clean data as they had hoped. Ancillary data collection activities (e.g., supplementary case studies, secondary data review) are often thrown aside in the end as time runs out. In a formal survey, your flexibility can be sharply limited once the questionnaires are designed and fielded and the sampling plan has been executed. You can often drop a few nonessential questions, but you are largely committed to the program once the survey is fielded. As one economist who fielded a formal survey reported, "A survey with a set body of questions and sampling scheme takes on a life of its own, and if the time and cost necessary are underestimated, it can be very hard to find room for cutting back." Hasty design and implementation of survey instruments have haunted many a social scientist as an unwieldy project dragged on long past the time when grant monies and the fieldworker's patience were exhausted.

Clearing the Decks

The last days and weeks in the field tend to be frantic. There is so much still to be done, and it is so important emotionally to achieve reasonable closure to an important chapter in your career and life. This is an intensely personal part of fieldwork, and can be very positive, as one researcher observed: "I think that last, frantic rush before departure is the beauty of the fieldwork experience. Making last-minute contacts, discovering sources and ideas that you wish you'd known months before, saying farewell to friends and to sights and sounds. It was a crucible in which many ideas and intuitions took form. Don't lament the anxiety, revel in it." Most fieldworkers seem to follow and recommend several steps.

The first dilemma you face is what to do with the scarce time remaining. Rest assured, triage is a necessary part of field research.

What do you really need to do that is also feasible? Gathering any remaining data unavailable at home usually falls into this category. At the same time, recognize that no one ever gets all the data they think they need, yet somehow good work gets done. Most fieldworkers develop an expansive sense of which materials are central to the project's success.

Nonetheless, dedicating all your time to data collection is generally not advisable. Data are rarely useful in the raw form in which fieldworkers collect them. Data need cleaning and organizing. This is an explicit part of the process in formal survey work, in which you must enter the data handwritten on questionnaires into some sort of computer database, then verify that the entered data make sense. When at all possible, enter the data into the computer software you intend to store and analyze it in before leaving the field. Rotating diskette backups is a common and wise precaution in this process. Entry and cleaning of field data at this stage permits return visits to the research site to correct errors inevitably identified during entry. Double- and triple-check the data, since returning to clean up misrecorded or poorly understood responses is far easier and cheaper when you are in the field than after you have returned home. The end result of field data entry and cleaning is generally a smoother transition from fieldwork to writeup. All the researchers consulted for this volume who finished their Ph.D.s within one year of their return home entered much, if not all, their data in the field, and in many cases began writing at the research site as well. Not only is your data more clearly organized, but you are already launched into analysis, so it becomes easier to advance rapidly after returning home (more on the transition back home in Chapter 8).

Many fieldworkers bring back far more data than they need for the current research project. This can be both a blessing and a curse. On the one hand, the seeds of the next project are already in hand, providing a natural excuse to remain in close contact with host country colleagues. Many of us find parting with newfound colleagues easier when we truly expect to be back soon, working together again. On the other hand, an abundance of data can be a dual burden: logistically, by having to move it all home safely, and intellectually, by taming your desire to master it all before sitting down to complete the initial project.

Many researchers we consulted indicated that they wanted to leave something tangible behind from their research. Some gave seminar presentations at their host research institution and at policy-making institutions before departure, disseminating preliminary research findings locally before polishing them up for presentation to the international academic community. Some host institutions have a working paper series for which you can write a synopsis of your findings as a still more lasting local legacy of your fieldwork. Better yet, you can deposit a copy of your field notes, data set, or both in a national research institute or library, being sure to inform other researchers where and how to access the material. Host country academics and policy-makers, not to mention future fieldworkers, can thereby benefit materially from your project.

For those doing survey work, it is a nice, but too rare, courtesy to present some basic findings in a simple closing talk to the subject community. This can provide useful feedback to the researcher as well

---

Closure with the Community

I got some additional funding to organize a day-long workshop, where my assistant and I presented some of our major findings, invited a couple of colleagues to comment on what we had done, and tried to generate some debate on the topic of our research. We invited other members of the research community, policy-makers and urban authorities, local political leaders, and a number of the people we had interviewed over the course of the year. . . . The dynamic of the ensuing debate was much different with a number of our respondents present. . . . The spectacle of a well-paid, well-fed expatriate researcher debating local authorities and policy-makers about informal economic practices brings to mind everything that is wrong about foreign researchers (the ivory tower syndrome, academic imperialism, etc.). The spectacle of low-income working women debating local authorities was altogether different, particularly when my data was essentially validating most of the claims the women were making vis-à-vis the authorities. Moreover, a number of the analytic insights resulting from that workshop were invaluable.

DAN MAXWELL

as to the subjects. Dan Maxwell went one step further in Uganda (see opposite).

You need not only to tie up loose ends with your research but also to attend to personal matters. Closing down your domestic arrangements can take some time. You must either transport home, give away, or sell accumulated household effects and research equipment. Since most returning fieldworkers are burdened with a Herculean load of research materials, local disposal or freight shipment home of any personal effects is often advisable. Obviously, you need to plan well ahead if trying to sell off larger items like a vehicle or a computer.

In some countries you need to pay attention to currency controls. In a probably futile effort to prevent capital flight, some countries restrict the amount of local currency you can take out of the country as well as the amount of local currency you can convert into hard (foreign) currency. In such places, you do not want to show up at the airport with a wad of bills that can neither be taken out (perhaps to be used on a subsequent return) nor converted to a currency useful at home. In this sort of monetary environment, it is wise to manage local currency holdings so as to have little or none left at the end.

Saying goodbye to friends, collaborators, assistants, and the community in which you resided or did research can be emotionally draining and time consuming. Be sensitive to prevailing local mores. In some cultures, failing to pay your respects immediately prior to departure is a serious slight frequently committed by businesslike westerners. Several respondents threw a party or offered a community gift as an expression of the bonds of mutual respect forged during the research period.

Packing Up the Data

The logistical feat of getting your research material home is unnervingly central to the whole intellectual endeavor of fieldwork. Months or years of painstaking work can vanish all too quickly if the proper precautions are not taken in packing and shipping your research materials. It pays to think carefully and early about how the data will get from the field site to wherever you plan to complete the analysis and writing, usually at home.

The first question concerns what to take home. Even if all your data have been entered into the computer, cleaned, and carefully reviewed, you should still keep the hard copy questionnaires and other documents. Marginal notes on questionnaires or passages not originally entered from documents may become important during the writeup of the project. All the research materials gathered in the field that cannot be found at home should go back, as should mementos, gifts for family and friends, and personal effects.

The second question concerns how to get everything home and what to do if your well-laid plans go awry. What will you do if the suitcase with all your questionnaires goes not to your destination but to the great luggage carousel in the sky? Take precautions against such low-probability but potentially catastrophic events. Although most fieldworkers never need the backup data sources they create, the peace of mind a backup provides is an important asset in itself. And on the rare occasions when your data are lost or damaged in transit, an effective insurance policy is invaluable.

There are two basic modes of data transport and contingency planning: electronic and physical. The electronic means are newer, not yet available in all corners of the world, and feasible only for data that can be put into a computer. Still, more than one scholar advised, "Whatever can be on a computer disk, should be." These are the most compact and cost-effective means of transporting data. Also, electronic data can often be sent ahead electronically or left behind in a site accessible electronically from home. One researcher regularly downloaded her data from Hong Kong to her home computer in the United States over the internet. Another left a copy of his data in a dedicated subdirectory on an internet-accessible computer at his host institution abroad. If he had lost his diskettes in transit, he could have used FTP (file transfer protocol on the internet) to bring a copy home electronically.

The more traditional, physical means of transporting data home can be expensive, including the cost of photocopying to insure against loss (more on this below) as well as excess baggage charges. Most first-time fieldworkers are shocked at how much STUFF they acquire in the field, and how expensive and cumbersome it is to ship. It is almost always worth the premium to send your research materials home by the safest possible means. Some send boxes of documents as unaccompanied baggage with a courier service or an airline. These services are usually good at tracking down lost items expeditiously. Be aware, however, that airline booking agents are often unfamiliar with the details of air freight, so it would behoove you to visit the airport freight office personally to work out details. The same holds true for seaborne freight in the unlikely event that you send data home by ship. On rare occasions, you can send materials home with family, friends, or colleagues returning early. Nevertheless, if you are inclined to ask others to help you, be sensitive that many people are rightly cautious about assuming responsibility for taking others' baggage across borders. Finally, if you are affiliated with the U.S. government in some way (as a Fulbright scholar, for example), inquire whether it will be possible to ship things home via the diplomatic pouch. One of the coauthors had the fortune to get in the good graces of a consular official and was able to ship back eleven boxes of heavy materials (paper and books) free of charge using the diplomatic pouch. However, if you do ship things home, keep in mind that someone must be waiting at the other end to accept the shipment when it arrives. As a consequence, you need to coordinate arrangements for receipt and storage of the material until you are able to claim the baggage yourself.

Most fieldworkers carry most, if not all, their research materials with them on the plane home. This works well for computer diskettes, which are light and compact. It does not always work as well for documents and physical specimens. The feasibility of accompanied baggage decreases precipitously, and the expense rises equally quickly, the greater the volume and weight of the materials being sent home. Remember that several boxes of documents can get incredibly heavy. One fellow made it through eighteen months' fieldwork in Sri Lanka without a single injury or illness to speak of, only to break his wrist at the airport at home as he wrestled a pile of overstuffed bags through customs in a severely jet-lagged state. At least one researcher thus recommended bringing along a couple of portable luggage dollies to help negotiate your small mountain of heavy luggage through customs checks and airports.

The day of departure often brings unwanted complications. Perhaps chief among these are conflicts with customs officials. Boxes of books, interview transcripts, and diskettes, may seem innocuous enough but sometimes raise the suspicions of security-minded customs agents. Especially if your research touches on areas of acute sensitivity in an authoritarian nation, it is unwise to count on a quick and simple clearance through customs. In a panic, some researchers are tempted to resort to bribery. We repeat the advice given in Chapter 4: Avoid bribes; they are usually a mistake. Quite aside from the serious ethical questions such actions raise, remember that some officials may interpret an offered bribe as confirmation that the customs agent has reason to be concerned about the contents under question. Thus, bribes are likely to backfire in these circumstances. Moreover, the too-conventional view of low- and middle-income countries as rife with corruption is often unfair and inaccurate. One researcher, reduced to bribing an airport porter in Los Angeles to clear overweight bags, found it an especially fitting end to his foreign research adventure: "Never a bribe mentioned or paid in Latin America, a land famous for corruption, but an 'enterprising' Los Angeles porter took me for a trip."

Whatever the means you choose to transport research materials home, it is wise to make copies, at least of irreplaceable original data, for temporary storage elsewhere. Duplication can consume enormous amounts of time, energy, money, and storage space. As a result, it often pays to find ways to minimize such redundancy. But you run very real risks if you try to save a bit of money by not making duplicate sets of irreplaceable materials. Many researchers leave a duplicate copy of irreplaceable data on site, in the hands of someone trustworthy, who can be contacted if your own copies do not make the trip home satisfactorily. If the data are not yet in final form, leave instructions to destroy the data after confirming the safe arrival home. Others mail a duplicate copy ahead, again relying on someone at home to care for the materials until you can reclaim them. Replaceable materials need not be duplicated if you ship them ahead early enough to verify their safe arrival before your own departure from the research site.

Finally, while it may be obvious, contingency planning should not wait until you are ready to leave for home. Prudent fieldworkers maintain current backup copies of their data. The laptop stolen from your dwelling or baggage is replaceable, but are the data or initial draft chapters resident on the hard drive? Rotating diskette backups and offsite storage of diskettes and photocopied primary documents provide an effective, if not always convenient, safeguard against calamity.

8

Pulling It All Together: The Postpartum

Fieldworkers anticipate some turbulence in settling into a strange place in the field, but few prepare themselves for the shock of reintroduction to the familiar but sometimes unfathomable place from whence they came. Return from the field can be a depressing, disorienting experience for some social scientists, a soul-searching time for many, and a nonevent for others. However you respond to the potential culture shock of returning home after intense months or years of fieldwork, you finally confront the need to pull the mass of data together into a manageable project. The initial months are often fraught with both organizational and emotional frustration, as well as the problems associated with becoming reaccustomed to the intellectual environment at home. In this chapter we deal with how to cope with the myriad problems of putting your work in a broader framework, organizing the data, and getting into writing.

Organizing Data

For some, the arrangement of data comes only with the process of writing, while for others data organization must precede writing. Most of our respondents fell into the latter group, although largely this is a matter of personal style and chosen research methodology. For those who must organize first, we again strongly suggest not waiting until returning from the field to begin putting data in order. Indeed, the daunting prospect of organizing the data often contributes to the pitfalls outlined in the introduction to this chapter. More than one researcher recommended merging the data analysis, writing, and background research processes as soon as possible. One scholar summed up: "It's crucial to begin writing as soon as possible, I think, because as you write, you find out what you really need to know from the data. And as you look at the data, you find out what you need to write—a dialectical process."

Many fieldworkers spend tireless weeks and months cleaning and reorganizing data files upon their return. Because data cleaning and coding rarely taxes your creative juices, this is often a good activity for the transition period of intellectual resettlement at your home institution. Moreover, the tedium of the process often drives you to start writing.

Data security is still important here. At least one returned fieldworker, still reeling from the elaborate precautions he took to safeguard his data before leaving the field, headed straight for the bank and deposited a copy of his data on diskette in a safe deposit box. Do not be lulled into complacency because the electricity supply at home is more reliable or the diskettes of better quality than in the field.

Beginning (and Completing) the Writing Process

In many ways the key part of fieldwork begins when you start writing. Until that point, the exercise is primarily one of individual enrichment. Once the writing begins, you are able to convert assembled data into a coherent story for a broader audience, making your field site accessible, through print, to the world. The opportunity to share with others what informants and respondents have shared with you is an uncommon one, and you bear a great obligation to tell these stories well and truthfully. For many of us, these fundamental truths about field research provide motivation enough to get writing.

Indeed, some researchers choose to start writing in the field and a few even do all of it there. However, although doing some writing in the field can help the broader project, most researchers need some distance between themselves and their site to gain the perspective necessary to find the patterns running through the various pieces of the research project puzzle. Moreover, few fieldwork projects are purely empirical. Most rest upon a theoretical superstructure and must be placed in a broader literature. The ideal is to find a balance between full integration of theory into your findings and a clumsy graft ex post facto. Too much writing in the field can lead to the latter.

Many returned fieldworkers find it difficult to start writing. In some cases, they are adrift in a sea of data. Returning to a central theme of this book, a well-organized prospectus or set of chapter outlines on a clearly circumscribed topic can enable you to find your bearings and get launched. Organizing and cleaning the data as you go along (in the field and at home) can also help in writing.

Still, the experience of fieldwork is often overwhelming, and it can take time for you to gain enough perspective on the work to be able to articulate and structure your findings in a coherent manner. Academic pursuits are by their nature somewhat lonesome, as long, hard hours of solitary data analysis, thought, organization, and writing drone on. Having another person around who knows the subject or the site intimately—a partner, a colleague, an adviser—can be a great boon, especially in the initial post-return period. Someone else quite familiar with the context, the data, or the issues at hand often helps you find a way to wade through the sea of materials you inevitably bring back from the field.

Motivation problems can be acute in the postfieldwork phase. Some researchers give themselves clear incentives, positive or negative, to begin and keep writing. Several researchers we consulted committed themselves to present a scholarly paper using their data at a professional conference shortly after their return. Others agreed to write a paper for a soon-to-be-published volume or a book review on a subject closely related to the topic of their field research. A sequence of related talks or papers beginning shortly after your return can provide the impetus and a firm schedule for writing the various chapters in your dissertation or monograph. This obviously works best if you started writing or at least scribbling a bit in the field, but even that is not essential. Pride and professional reputation can be powerful motivating instruments; harness them.

For many dissertators, the need to find a job inspires disciplined and rapid writing. This seems especially true for those who are supporting families and thus perhaps feel a more acute need to move to the next stage. The job search, especially for academic postings, requires reasonable progress on your work and often a fairly polished paper to offer. The incentives provided by a commitment to present findings from your fieldwork are thus effectively nested within the incentives laid out by throwing yourself into the job market. Keep in

---

Motivating Oneself to Write

[Writing up] is actually the most painful part of the whole process. It took me a year to figure out that I couldn't get going on writing up my dissertation if I tried to hold down a job at the same time. So, against the advice of everybody I knew, I quit and took out a year's worth of loans. That was a very good decision. Writing up can be tremendously difficult because the dissertation is so big that it's difficult to conceptualize it, let alone know where to start. Taking out loans worked because I couldn't afford to live on debt for more than a year, and so that's exactly how long I gave myself to finish it.

MARY CLARK

---

mind, however, that a job search is a more pressured undertaking. Do not underestimate the time, energy, and emotion tied up in the search for permanent employment. A job search can stimulate your productivity in finishing off the research project, but it can also take valuable time away from writing. Search for a judicious balance between these two and consult with advisers and loved ones to get input on whether you are ready.

Another motivational strategy, albeit a high-risk one, is to borrow money to support yourself during the writeup phase. Although many of us know of people who were compelled by debts coming due to accept full-time employment before they were ready, putting them on a degenerative spiral, incurring debts can terrify others into remarkable productivity, as Mary Clark recounts above.

Most returned fieldworkers begin by writing methodology chapters, bibliographies, lists of data sources, and other detail-intensive accounts from the field, later moving toward more theoretical components of the project. This sequencing serves three useful purposes. First, you can put down on paper important and too-often unrecorded details before time and distance conspire to erase them from your memory. Second, in the initial period back home, the fieldwork experience is familiar, while theory, which most people broadly ignore in the field, seems more alien. In the early weeks back, when simple things from daily life—going to the grocery store, reading the newspaper—are often discomforting, there is much to be said for working on material with which you feel (at least temporarily) more comfortable. Third, chapters on field methods, data sources, and descriptive statistics of your data can often be knocked out fairly quickly, giving you a sense of accomplishment and momentum toward the more difficult writing still ahead. Such simple psychological tricks appear repeatedly in researchers' accounts of how they prepared themselves to write up their projects.

Culture Shock

Just as you need time to adjust to life in the field, so too do many returned fieldworkers require some time to reacclimate themselves to life at home. Simply put, many experience culture shock at home. Some long desperately to get back on the plane and return to their research site, never to return home again, while others pick up where they left off as if there had never been an interruption. Your emotional response to returning home is a highly individual experience.

Reassimilation can be difficult, in extreme cases even temporarily paralyzing. Peoples' behaviors, the climate, the language, the smells, the food are all different and not necessarily better or more comfortable. Most likely this is a sign of how substantial the fieldwork experience was, a sure indication that you really need to start writing about it. If it is powerful enough to disorient you in your own home, it deserves reporting. The culture shock many feel on reintroduction to home also demonstrates that while fieldwork is explicitly an experience of discovery about some distant place, it is implicitly, but not always subtly, an experience of discovery about things and people quite close, not least about yourself. Often we allow ourselves months or years to process discoveries about our research site(s) but do not permit ourselves even a day to mull over and process what we have learned about ourselves or our homes. This can create a debilitating disequilibrium, to which the best antidote is often to relax, realize such sensations are not uncommon, write about them, and wait it out (and waiting is a practice to which all veteran fieldworkers grow accustomed!).

Although the professional side of virtually all scientists yearns to hit the ground running at home, this is simply not always possible. Culture shock or personal responsibilities may necessitate a hiatus from the project. For example, one of the coauthors took a two-month break to spend time with his pregnant wife and two children after returning from a three-month unaccompanied research trip abroad. Such breaks seem far more common, and perhaps far more sensible, than is acknowledged in the halls of academe. Just as good field research cannot be rushed and must advance in equilibrium with your personal acclimatization, so too must postfieldwork analysis and writeup proceed deliberately, not hastily. By all means, set about the task of writing, but not at all costs. With luck, your fieldwork experience will be the beginning of a long and fruitful relationship with your site and, more broadly, the practice of fieldwork.

9

Epilogue: It's Never Over

This book is meant to prepare the researcher for the challenges and joys of fieldwork to help make the entire process more fruitful. Nevertheless, the narrative would not be complete if we considered a fieldwork project as a discrete event in your life. For many researchers, fieldwork becomes almost addictive, and an initial experience is the start of a career punctuated by substantial periods in the field. But even when you do not obtain or pursue further opportunities to embark on new international projects, time spent in intensive research overseas invariably has durable effects. In this epilogue we briefly discuss some of the postfieldwork obligations and opportunities that most researchers will confront after they come home.

Postfieldwork Obligations

As anyone who has ever gone to the field knows, the researcher takes a great deal home that represents enormous contributions by others: survey data that required hundreds of hours of time from respondents; interview transcripts, tapes, or notes resulting from the time donated by busy people; archival materials stored and often organized by people in the field. The relationship between the researcher and the researched is often asymmetrical, and as a researcher, you should do whatever possible to return something to those in the field after you have left. As one contributor said, "I think it is very important to be more than a fleeting presence in a community which one expects to gain some knowledge of. The information belongs there since it is there that it may truly be useful. And it is my responsibility to establish within my means the opportunity for people involved to question or respond to my ideas and conclusions."

At the very least, of course, do no harm to your informants. We have already addressed some of the issues associated with informant and respondent anonymity and confidentiality in Chapter 6. Regarding interviews, we repeat the need to do everything in your power to protect informants. Some contributors have also had to be very careful with protecting sources for other kinds of data they have collected. One political scientist, who did archival research, reported:

> My written data exists in a huge gray area. The archivists who
> provided it to me were uneasy about doing so, but laid down no
> clear guidelines for its use. I feel an ethical obligation to them
> to maintain some level of vagueness as to the source of the doc-
> uments (for example, quoting a document and suggesting that
> it is in the personal papers of a high-level government official
> without naming the official, much as I do with the interviews).
> I also feel obligated to future researchers to make sure I am very
> careful in the ways in which I incorporate sensitive material. If
> I use it in a more polemical fashion, or without explaining the
> full context of the quotes, then I may endanger future access to
> these documents.

Protecting sources not only safeguards informants against persecution, but may make scholarship easier for those who follow in your footsteps. Exercise careful judgment over what to do with collected information since informants may not realize the implications of the research project. Which information and identities are and are not sensitive often changes over time, sometimes dramatically and in ways unforeseen by the researcher. It is prudent and considerate to err on the side of caution.

If you conduct formal surveys, you also need to be concerned about your data sources, and come up with ways of protecting your sources if you plan to share data with others. One economist wrote that he would "release the data for broader distribution identified only by number, with a separate key containing identifying information only for those researchers who will need to reinterview or match records, possibly asking for a statement agreeing to certain terms of use." As he pointed out, you must be very careful in deciding with whom to share data. He also recommended adding "noise" to some variables in the "unidentified" data set to make sure that individual respondents cannot be identified without consulting the researcher.

Beyond protecting informants, the most tangible and universal obligation is to report accurately and fully what you have learned. Unlike theoretical or conceptual work, in which no one researcher has superior access to the ideas or disciplinary tools necessary to replicate findings, and unlike discourse within the studied community, in which others equally familiar with the issue and the context in which it has been studied can challenge findings, the empirical researcher writing up results at home operates in a sort of safe haven. Findings may be based upon data to which others do not immediately have access, and some of which may not be transferable (e.g., sensitive information or unrecorded impressions). Because overseas data collection is an expensive exercise, you bear an obligation to both the scientific and host communities to make data available when at all possible for the purposes of replication and extension.

Most scholars recommend the common practice of sending unpublished or published research results to individuals and institutions in the field. One economist described some more creative means of sharing her data:

> At the village level, I left behind charts and diagrams summarizing the mean statistics on work and income in that community. For academics and policy-makers, I gave two public talks before leaving the field, and I wrote a working paper for the university graduate program, which was printed up and distributed a few months after I left the field. In a followup trip to Honduras I revisited three communities to followup with enumerators.

Others—especially those working on collaborative projects—will have more formal obligations to share the results of their research.

Sharing data and findings can also lead to possibilities of coauthorship of articles or papers with fellow academics in the field. This can be satisfying for both the researcher and the local academic and is one of the few ways in which the host/researcher relationship can approximate an equal exchange. As one researcher emphasized, "It is essential that researchers realize the importance of treating interviewees and informants as colleagues rather than as simple subjects." Collaboration is one of the best ways to put such a sentiment into

---

Fieldwork as an Ongoing Process

I became rather closely involved with the trade union community in particular in Namibia and with many Namibians in general. I feel that I will have an ongoing relationship with both well into the future. I came to work with the trade unions as a researcher doing research on them but I also worked for them as we grappled with the trade unions' own research capacity in an independent Namibia. In such situations one should always be careful not to promise more than one can deliver. One should never make any commitments that one does not intend to or cannot fill. To do so would be to enhance people's expectations falsely and would be very wrong. At this early stage I am not exactly sure how my relationship with the trade unionists and other informants will develop in the future. In large part this is because of the way in which the whole issue of the trade unions has become so politicized and the way in which any foreigners who might be attempting to influence the trade unions (e.g., to disaffiliate from the ruling party) are being viewed by the authorities. For the time being, I feel that I need to move away from the unions and perhaps attempt other research in Namibia.

GRETCHEN BAUER

---

practice, since both the local and foreign researcher will produce something tangible, each using his or her particular strengths, contacts, and accumulated knowledge.

A word of caution is in order at this point. Although you may want to share your research, contacts, and resources with those with whom you work in the field, be careful about making promises, whether academic or financial. Furthermore, as Gretchen Bauer notes above, future relationships with informants can become complicated after you leave the field, especially when you had close contact with the research subjects. In particular, political factors might limit what you can do in the future.

Bauer underlines the point that the researcher should regard the fieldwork as an ongoing process and not a one-shot deal.

Postfieldwork Opportunities

While fieldwork encumbers you with obligations to do no harm to informants and respondents, to report stories accurately and fully, and to make data available to the broader scientific community, it also provides uncommon personal and professional opportunities. They include the social opportunities associated with new and often lifelong friendships. They also involve numerous professional opportunities, ranging from the possibility of advising others as an "expert" on your research topic to opportunities to expand further on your original research project, either in the same country or elsewhere. In short, overseas social science research pays permanent dividends to those blessed with the chance to do it. We hasten to add that one may see obligations turn into opportunities, for example, with the chance to coauthor an article with a researcher from your fieldsite.

Ken Wilson (1993, 198) succinctly summarized several of the most important and tangible benefits of fieldwork:

> Fieldwork is for life. Friendships and responsibilities are created that will stay with you forever. Many researchers still correspond with people from the area they worked in decades later. Several have made follow-up studies, a re-engagement that catapulted them back into the personal relationships of previous years. A few researchers have never made the break and ended up abandoning academia altogether and going back to live with the people they studied.

Opportunities for consultancies or contract research often appear following an intensive fieldwork period overseas. Research institutions and policy-makers value experience. No matter how ignorant you might feel when you return home overwhelmed with data and impressions gathered but not fully analyzed or synthesized in the field, an astonishing number of people rightly label returned fieldworkers "experts" in the area. You may be able to take advantage of this newly acquired status. For example, one scholar we spoke with parlayed her dissertation fieldwork experience into an opportunity to go back to "her" country on a USAID mission. Upon her return to the field, she was able to renew old contacts and verify and refine some of her earlier conclusions.

Many scholars use their field experience to begin new research projects. Often, such extensions involve research in neighboring countries

and allow a more comparative project with potentially broader implications, in which you ask similar research questions in a different context. Having proven you could execute the research in one place
makes you less of a risk for potential funders. Therefore, emphasize
previous research experience when attempting to secure new funding.
You can also use field contacts to begin a new project on a related
theme. For example, one of the coauthors used his initial experience
in Brazil studying trade policy as a stepping stone for a broader research project on South American economic integration. The initial
research experience made this new project possible. It provided contacts, knowledge of resources, and a familiarity with the local context
that made it possible to ask more appropriate research questions.

Finally, you can return to the field to do followup research in the
same site. Longitudinal studies over the span of many years are quite
rare in the social sciences. The ability to return to a site and replicate
a study after the passage of time is a methodological option unavailable to most social scientists. If done right, this can be an extremely
valuable intellectual contribution.

Overseas fieldwork is a complicated and challenging process. Some
of the challenges are random and unique, depending on the particu-
larities of individual countries; others are predictable. In this book we
have concentrated on the latter, operating on the premise that fieldwork will go much more smoothly if you take steps to prepare for
some typical challenges. As we noted in the introduction, the fieldwork process is a (sometimes absurd!) sequence of decision points. We
have tried, in this book, to give you the benefit of the substantial experience of many who have already gone through the process, through
the difficulties, and through the satisfaction of the truly rare experience of going abroad and trying to understand a foreign culture.

Selected Bibliography

In this selected bibliography we provide a broad compendium, not a comprehensive listing, of relevant materials on social science fieldwork in developing countries. Many of the references were taken from the "recommended readings" bibliography prepared for the Social Science Research Council's International Predissertation Fellowship Program. Other references were provided by the coauthors, contributors, and others who reviewed the manuscript.

Archival Research

Elder, G. H. et al. 1993. *Working with Archival Data: Studying Lives.* Newbury Park, Calif.: Sage Publications.

Hill, M. R. 1993. *Archival Strategies and Techniques.* Newbury Park, Calif.: Sage Publications.

Scott, J. 1990. *A Matter of Record: Documentary Sources in Social Research.* Cambridge, Mass.: Basil Blackwell.

Weeks, J. M. 1991. *Introduction to Library Research in Anthropology.* Boulder, Colo.: Westview Press.

Westerman, R. C. 1994. *Fieldwork in the Library: A Guide to Research in Anthropology and Related Area Studies.* Chicago, Ill.: American Library Association.

Case Study Research and Comparative Method

Achen, C., and D. Snidal. 1989. "Rational Deterrence Theory and Comparative Case Studies." *World Politics* 41:143–69.

Dogan, M., and D. Pelassy. 1984. *How to Compare Nations: Strategies in Comparative Politics.* Chatham, N.J.: Chatham House Publishers.

Eckstein, H. 1975. "Case Study and Theory in Political Science." In F. I. Greenstein and N. W. Polsby, eds., *Strategies of Inquiry*, Reading, Mass.: Addison-Wesley.

Geddes, B. 1990. "How the Cases You Choose Affect the Answers You Get: Selection Bias in Comparative Politics." *Political Analysis* 2:131–49.

Lieberson, S. 1991. "Small N's and Big Conclusions: An Examination of the Reasoning in Comparative Studies Based on a Small N of Cases." *Social Forces* 70:307–20.

Lijphart, A. 1975. "The Comparable-Cases Strategy in Comparative Research." *Comparative Political Studies* 8:158–77.

Ragin, C. 1987. *The Comparative Method.* Berkeley: University of California Press.

Tilly, C. 1984. *Big Structures, Large Processes, Huge Comparisons.* New York: Russell Sage Foundation.

Yin, R. K. 1988. *Case Study Research: Design and Methods.* Newbury Park, Calif.: Sage Publications.

Ethnographic Methods and Research on Human Subjects

Agar, M. 1980. *The Professional Stranger: An Informal Introduction to Ethnography.* New York: Academic Press.

Asad, J. 1973. *Anthropology and the Colonial Encounter.* New York: Humanities Press.

Barley, N. 1983. *The Innocent Anthropologist.* London: British Museum Publications.

Barnes, J. A. 1979. *Who Should Know What? Social Science, Privacy, and Ethics.* New York and Cambridge: Cambridge University Press.

Bartis, P. 1990. *Folklife and Fieldwork: A Layman's Introduction to Field Techniques,* rev. ed. Washington, D.C.: Library of Congress.

Bell, D., P. Caplan, and W. J. Karim, eds. 1993. *Gendered Fields: Women, Men, and Ethnography.* London and New York: Routledge.

Brown, R. H., ed. 1992. *Writing the Social Text: Poetics and Politics in Social Science Discourse.* New York: A. de Gruyter.

Burgess, R., ed. 1982. *Field Research: A Source Book and Field Manual.* New York: Routledge Chapman and Hall.

Clifford, J., and G. E. Marcus. 1986. *Writing Culture: The Poetics and Politics of Ethnography.* Berkeley: University of California Press.

Devereux, S. 1993. "'Observers Are Worried': Learning the Language and Counting the People in Northeast Ghana." In S. Devereux and J. Hoddinott, eds., *Fieldwork in Developing Countries.* Boulder, Colo.: Lynne Rienner.

Dexter, L. 1970. *Elite and Specialized Interviewing.* Evanston, Ill.: Northwestern University Press.

Douglas, J. D. 1985. *Creative Interviewing.* Beverly Hills: Sage Publications.

Ellen, R. F. 1984. *Ethnographic Research: A Guide to General Conduct.* New York: Academic Press.

Ely, M. 1991. *Doing Qualitative Research: Circles within Circles.* London and New York: Falmer Press.

Emerson, R. M., R. I. Fretz, and L. L. Shaw. 1995. *Writing Ethnographic Fieldnotes.* Chicago: University of Chicago Press.

Finnegan, R. H. 1992. *Oral Traditions and the Verbal Arts: A Guide to Research Practices.* London and New York: Routledge.

Fox, R. G. 1991. *Recapturing Anthropology: Working in the Present.* Santa Fe: School of American Research Press (distributed by University of Washington Press).

Geertz, C. 1988. *Works and Lives: The Anthropologist as Author.* Stanford, Calif.: Stanford University Press.

Gladwin, C. H. 1989. *Ethnographic Decision Tree Modeling.* Newbury Park, Calif.: Sage Publications.

Golde, P., ed. 1986. *Women in the Field: Anthropological Experiences,* 2d ed. Berkeley: University of California Press.

Gravel, P. B., and R. B. M. Ridinger. 1988. *Anthropological Fieldwork: An Annotated Bibliography.* New York: Garland Press.

Hammersley, M. 1995. *Ethnography: Principles in Practice,* 2d ed. London and New York: Routledge.

Ives, E. D. 1995. *The Tape-Recorded Interview: A Manual for Field Workers in Folklore and Oral History,* 2d ed. Knoxville: University of Tennessee Press.

Jackson, B. 1987. *Fieldwork.* Urbana: University of Illinois Press.

Jorgensen, D. L. 1989. *Participant Observation: A Methodology for Human Studies.* Newbury Park, Calif.: Sage Publications.

Lee, R. M. 1995. *Dangerous Fieldwork.* Thousand Oaks, Calif.: Sage Publications.

Malinowski, B. 1989 [1967]. *A Diary in the Strict Sense of the Term.* Stanford, Calif.: Stanford University Press.

Moran, E. F. 1995. *The Comparative Analysis of Human Societies: Toward Common Standards for Data Collection and Reporting.* Boulder, Colo.: Lynne Rienner.

Moris, J., and J. Copestake. 1993. *Qualitative Enquiry for Rural Development: A Review.* London: Intermediate Technology Publications, Overseas Development Institute.

Nordstrom, C., and A. C. G. M. Robben. 1995. *Fieldwork under Fire: Contemporary Studies of Violence and Survival.* Berkeley: University of California Press.

Panini, M. N., ed. 1991. *From the Female Eye: Accounts of Women Fieldworkers Studying their Own Communities.* Delhi: Hindustan Publishing.

Pelto, G., and P. Pelto. 1978. *Anthropological Research: The Structure of Inquiry,* 2d ed. New York: Cambridge University Press.

Pfohl, J. 1986. *Participatory Evaluation: A User's Guide.* New York: PACT Publications.

Punch, M. 1986. *The Politics and Ethics of Fieldwork.* Newbury Park, Calif.: Sage Publications.

Rosaldo, M., and L. Lamphere. 1974. *Woman, Culture, and Society.* Stanford, Calif.: Stanford University Press.

Rosaldo, R. 1993. *Culture and Truth: The Remaking of Social Analysis.* Boston: Beacon Press.

Sanjek, R. 1990. *Fieldnotes: The Makings of Anthropology.* Ithaca, N.Y.: Cornell University Press.

Schoepfle, M., and O. Werner. 1987. *Systematic Fieldwork.* Newbury Park, Calif.: Sage Publications.

Shaffir, W. B., and R. A. Stebbins, eds. 1991. *Experiencing Fieldwork: An Inside View of Qualitative Research.* Newbury Park, Calif.: Sage Publications.

Spradley, J. P. 1979. *The Ethnographic Interview.* New York: Holt, Rinehart and Winston.

———. 1980. *Participant Observation.* New York: Holt, Rinehart and Winston.

Stocking, G. W., Jr. 1983. *Observers Observed: Essays on Ethnographic Fieldwork.* Madison: University of Wisconsin Press.

Stouthamer-Loeber, M., and W. B. van Kammen. 1995. *Data Collection and Management: A Practical Guide.* Thousand Oaks, Calif.: Sage Publications.

Van Maanen, J. 1988. *Tales of the Field: On Writing Ethnography.* Chicago: University of Chicago Press.

———, ed. 1995. *Representation in Ethnography.* Thousand Oaks, Calif.: Sage Publications.

Warren, C. A. B. 1988. *Gender Issues in Field Research.* Newbury Park, Calif.: Sage Publications.

Whitehead, T. L., and M. E. Conaway, eds. 1986. *Self, Sex, and Gender in Cross-Cultural Fieldwork.* Urbana: University of Illinois Press.

Zamora, M. D., and B. B. Erring, eds. 1986. *Human Intervention: Fieldwork in Cultural Anthropology.* Trondheim, Norway: Dept. of Social Anthropology, University of Trondheim (publication of the Association of Third World Anthropologists).

Fieldwork in General

Ackroyd, S., and J. A. Hughes. 1981. *Data Collection in Context.* London: Longman.

Barley, N. 1983. *The Innocent Anthropologist: Notes from a Mud Hut.* New York: Penguin.

Barnes, J. A. 1977. *The Ethics of Inquiry in Social Science.* Oxford: Oxford University Press.

Bauer, D. G. 1995. *The "How To" Grants Manual.* Phoenix: Oryx Press.

Burgess, R. G. 1984. *In the Field: An Introduction to Field Research.* Boston: George Allen & Unwin.

Devereux, S., and J. Hoddinott, eds. 1993. *Fieldwork in Developing Countries.* Boulder, Colo.: Lynne Rienner.

DeVita, P. R. 1992. *The Naked Anthropologist: Tales from Around the World.* Belmont, Calif.: Wadsworth Publishing.

Freilich, M., ed. 1977. *Marginal Natives at Work: Anthropologists in the Field.* New York: John Wiley & Sons.

Golden, M. P., ed. 1976. *The Research Experience.* Itasca, Ill.: F. E. Peacock.

Myrdal, G. 1969. *Objectivity in Social Research.* New York: Pantheon Books.

Penslar, R. L. 1994. *Research Ethics: Cases and Materials.* Bloomington: Indiana University Press.

Rabinow, P. 1977. *Reflections on Fieldwork in Morocco.* Berkeley: University of California Press.

Razavi, S. 1993. "Fieldwork in a Familiar Setting: The Role of Politics at the National, Community, and Household Levels." In S. Devereux and J. Hoddinott, eds., *Fieldwork in Developing Countries.* Boulder, Colo.: Lynne Rienner.

Smith, C. D., and W. Kornblum, eds. 1989. *In the Field: Readings on the Field Research Experience.* New York: Praeger.

Whitehead, T. L., and M. E. Conway. 1986. *Self, Sex, and Gender in Cross-Cultural Fieldwork.* Urbana: University of Illinois Press.

Wilson, K. 1993. "Thinking about the Ethics of Fieldwork." In S. Devereux and J. Hoddinott, eds., *Fieldwork in Developing Countries.* Boulder, Colo.: Lynne Rienner.

Living Abroad

Albright, S., A. Chu, and L. Austin. 1993. *Moving and Living Abroad: A Complete Handbook for Families,* rev. S. Albright and C. deKay Wilson. New York: Hippocrene Books.

Cassell, J. 1987. *Children in the Field: Anthropological Experiences.* Philadelphia: Temple University Press.

Kohls, L. R. 1995. *Survival Kit for Overseas Living: For Americans Planning to Live and Work Abroad.* Yarmouth, Maine: Intercultural Press.

Rose, S. R. 1994. *International Travel Health Guide.* Northhampton, Mass.: Travel Medicine (annual publication).

Schroeder, D. G. 1993. *Staying Healthy in Asia, Africa, and Latin America,* 3d ed. Chico, Calif.: Moon Publications.

U.S. Department of State. 1994. *Security Guidelines for American Families Living Abroad.* Washington, D.C.: U.S. Dept. of State, Overseas Security Advisory Council.

Weller, C. N. 1995. *The Overseas Assignment: A Professional's Guide for Working in Developing Countries.* Tulsa, Okla.: PennWell Books.

Werner, D., with C. Thuman and J. Maxwell. 1992. *Where There Is No Doctor.* Palo Alto, Calif.: Hesperian Foundation.

Quantitative Methods

Agresti, A., and B. Finlay. 1986. *Statistical Methods for the Social Sciences.* Riverside, N.J.: Dellen/Macmillan Publishing.

Amemiya, T. 1987. *Advanced Econometrics.* Cambridge: Harvard University Press.

Berndt, E. 1991. *The Practice of Econometrics, Classic and Contemporary.* Reading, Mass.: Addison-Wesley.

Box, G. E. P., and G. M. Jenkins. 1984. *Time Series Analysis: Forecasting and Control,* 2d ed. San Francisco: Holden Day.

Dixon, P. B., et al. 1992. *Notes and Problems in Applied General Equilibrium Economics.* New York: New Holland.

Dubois, J.-L. 1992. *Think before Measuring: Methodological Innovation for the Collection and Analysis of Statistical Data.* Washington, D.C.: World Bank.

Ethridge, D. 1995. *Research Methodology in Applied Economics: Understanding, Planning, and Conducting Economic Research.* Ames: Iowa State University Press.

Freedman, D., R. Pisani, R. Purves, and A. Adhikari. 1991. *Statistics,* 2d ed. New York: Norton.

Gebremedhin, T. G., and L. G. Tweeten. 1994. *Research Methods and Communication in the Social Sciences.* Westport, Conn.: Praeger.

Greene, W. 1990. *Econometric Analysis.* New York: Macmillan.

Harvey, A. 1990. *The Econometric Analysis of Time Series.* New York: Philip Plan.

Hoel, P. 1984. *Introduction to Mathematical Statistics,* 5th ed. New York: Wiley.

Judge, G. G., et al. 1988. *Introduction to the Theory and Practice of Econometrics,* 2d ed. New York: Wiley.

Nachmias, D., and C. Nachmias. 1987. *Research Methods in the Social Sciences,* 3d ed. New York: St. Martin's Press.

Neuman, W. L. 1994. *Social Research Methods: Qualitative and Quantitative Approaches.* Boston: Allyn & Bacon.

Survey Research

Ashby, J. A. 1990. *Evaluating Technology with Farmers: A Handbook.* Cali, Colombia: CIAT.

Belbase, K. P. 1991. "Rural Household Data Collection in Developing Countries: Designing Instruments for Collecting General Household Information Data." Cornell University Working Paper in Agricultural Economics 91-13. Ithaca, N.Y.

Booker, W., P. Singh, and L. Savane. 1980. "Household Survey Experience in Africa." Living Standards Measurement Study Working Paper 6. Washington, D.C.: World Bank.

Casley, D. J., and D. A. Lury. 1981. *Data Collection in Developing Countries.* Oxford: Oxford University Press.

Converse, J., and S. Presser. 1986. *Survey Questions: Handcrafting the Standardized Questionnaire.* Beverly Hills, Calif.: Sage Publications.

Freedman, D., et al. 1988. "The Life History Calendar: A Technique for Collecting Retrospective Data." In *Sociological Methodology,* vol. 18, pp. 37–68. San Francisco: Jossey-Bass.

Grootaert, C. 1982. "The Conceptual Basis of Measures of Household Welfare and Their Implied Survey Data Requirements." Living Standards Measurement Study Working Paper 19. Washington, D.C.: World Bank.

Grootaert, C., and K. F. Cheung. 1985. "Household Expenditure Surveys: Some Methodological Issues." Living Standards Measurement Study Working Paper 22. Washington, D.C.: World Bank.

Johnson, A. C., Jr., and J. S. Rowe. 1987. *Agricultural Statistics for Developing Countries.* Madison: University of Wisconsin.

Kalton, G. 1986. *Introduction to Survey Sampling.* Beverly Hills: Sage Publications.

Kiecolt, K. J., and L. E. Nathan. 1985. *Secondary Analysis of Survey Data.* Sage University Paper, Quantitative Applications in the Social Sciences No. 07-053.

Kumar, K. 1989. "Conducting Key Informant Interviews in Developing Countries." USAID Program Design and Evaluation Methodology Report 13. Washington, D.C.: USAID.

Leones, J. P. 1991. "Rural Household Data Collection in Developing Countries: Designing Instruments and Methods for Collecting Time Allocation Data." Cornell University Working Paper in Agricultural Economics 91-16. Ithaca, N.Y.

Leones, J. P., and S. Rozelle. 1991. "Rural Household Data Collection in Developing Countries: Designing Instruments and Methods for Collecting Off-Farm Income Data." Cornell University Working Paper in Agricultural Economics 91-18. Ithaca, N.Y.

Levin, C. 1991. "Rural Household Data Collection in Developing Countries: Designing Instruments and Methods for Collecting Consumption and Expenditure Data." Cornell University Working Paper in Agricultural Economics 91-14. Ithaca, N.Y.

Lipton, M., and M. Moore. 1972. "The Methodology of Village Studies in Less Developed Countries." Discussion Paper Number 10. Sussex, Eng.: Institute of Development Studies.

Longhurst, R. 1981. "Research Methodology and Rural Economy in Northern Nigeria." In *IDS Bulletin,* vol. 12, pp. 23–31. Sussex, Eng.: Institute of Development Studies.

Low, J. W. 1991. "Rural Household Data Collection in Developing Countries: Designing Instruments and Methods for Collecting Health and Nutrition Data." Cornell University Working Paper in Agricultural Economics 91-15. Ithaca, N.Y.

Poate, C. D., and P. F. Daplyn. 1993. *Data for Agrarian Development.* Cambridge: Cambridge University Press.

Randolph, T. 1991. "Rural Household Data Collection in Developing Countries: Preparing the Data for Analysis." Cornell University Working Paper in Agricultural Economics 91-19. Ithaca, N.Y.

Rossi, P., J. D. Wright, and A. B. Anderson. 1983. *Handbook of Survey Research.* Orlando, Fla.: Academic Press.

Rozelle, S. 1991. "Rural Household Data Collection in Developing Countries: Designing Instruments and Methods for Collecting Farm Production Data." Cornell University Working Paper in Agricultural Economics 91-17. Ithaca, N.Y.

Scott, C., P. T. A. de Andre, and R. Chander. 1980. "Conducting Surveys in Developing Countries: Practical Problems and Experience in Brazil, Malaysia, and the Philippines." Living Standards Measurement Study Working Paper 5. Washington, D.C.: World Bank.

Sudman, S., and N. M. Bradburn. 1982. *Asking Questions: A Practical Guide to Questionnaire Design.* San Francisco: Jossey-Bass.

Tatian, P. A. 1992. *Designing a Data Entry and Verification System.* Washington, D.C.: International Food Policy Research Institute.

Von Braun, J., and D. Puetz, eds. 1993. *Data Need for Food Policy in Developing Countries: New Directions for Household Surveys.* Washington, D.C.: International Food Policy Research Institute.

Weisberg, H., and B. D. Bowen. 1977. *An Introduction to Survey Research and Data Analysis.* San Francisco: W. H. Freeman.

Wood, G. D., Jr., and J. A. Knight. 1985. "The Collection of Price Data for the Measurement of Living Standards." Living Standards Measurement Study Working Paper 21. Washington, D.C.: World Bank.

Contributors

HELEN RUTH ASPAAS is an assistant professor of geography and earth resources at Utah State University.

PATRICK BARRETT is a Ph.D. candidate in political science at the University of Wisconsin–Madison.

GRETCHEN BAUER is an assistant professor of political science and international relations at the University of Delaware.

CAROLYN BEHRMAN is a Ph.D. candidate in anthropology at the University of Pennsylvania.

KAREN BOOTH is a Ph.D. candidate in sociology at the University of Wisconsin–Madison.

STEVE BOUCHER is a Ph.D. candidate in agricultural economics at the University of Wisconsin–Madison.

SUSAN BURGERMAN is a Ph.D. candidate in political science at Columbia University.

MARY CLARK is an assistant professor of political science at Tulane University.

LISA FISCHLER is a Ph.D. candidate in political science at the University of Wisconsin–Madison.

ARMANDO GUEVARA-GIL is a Ph.D. candidate in anthropology at the University of Wisconsin–Madison.

LAURA HAMMOND is a Ph.D. candidate in anthropology at the University of Wisconsin–Madison.

SOREN HAUGE is a Ph.D. candidate in economics at the University of Wisconsin–Madison.

DARREN HAWKINS is a Ph.D. candidate in political science at the University of Wisconsin–Madison.

FRANCISCA JAMES-HERNANDEZ is a Ph.D. candidate in anthropology at Stanford University.

ELIZABETH KATZ is an assistant professor of economics at Barnard College.

DAN MAXWELL is a postdoctoral fellow with the International Food Policy Research Institute.

WALTER MOLANO is vice president and economist for Latin America at CS First Boston Corporation.

TYLER PRIEST is a Ph.D. candidate in history at the University of Wisconsin–Madison.

WILL RENO is an assistant professor of political science at Florida International University.

CHUCK SCHMITZ is a Ph.D. candidate in geography at the University of California–Berkeley.

JERRY SHIVELY is an assistant professor of environmental and natural resource economics at Purdue University.

DENISE STANLEY is an assistant professor of economics at the University of Tennessee–Knoxville.

MICHAEL SULLIVAN is a Ph.D. candidate in political science at the University of Wisconsin–Madison.

AILI TRIPP is an assistant professor of political science and women's studies at the University of Wisconsin–Madison.

MERLE WALLACE is a Ph.D. candidate in educational psychology at the University of Illinois.

GREG WHITE is an assistant professor of government at Smith College.

Index

SOCIAL SCIENCE LIBRARY

Oxford University Library Services
Manor Road
Oxford OX1 3UQ
Tel: (2)71093 (enquiries and renewals)
http://www.ssl.ox.ac.uk

This is a NORMAL LOAN item.

We will email you a reminder before this item is due.

Please see http://www.ssl.ox.ac.uk/lending.html
for details on:

- loan policies; these are also displayed on the
notice boards and in our library guide.

- how to check when your books are due back.

- how to renew your books, including information
on the maximum number of renewals.
Items may be renewed if not reserved by
another reader. Items must be renewed before
the library closes on the due date.

- level of fines; fines are charged on overdue books.

Please note that this item may be recalled during Term.

WITHDRAWN

"An outstanding introduction to the practical issues that inevitably confront academics engaged in field research outside the United States."—Kent Worcester, Social Science Research Council

"I cannot imagine a better source of useful ideas and wisdoms for avoiding those problems which can be avoided, and for dealing practically with those which cannot. I will keep a supply of *Overseas Research* on hand as the perfect gift to aspiring field researchers."—Michael R. Carter, University of Wisconsin

Scholars and students engaged in overseas research projects often spend much of their time worrying about mundane details never reported in published research. In fact, the quality of scholarship often depends on the researcher's ability to navigate a bewildering array of social, financial, bureaucratic, and logistical obstacles encountered in preparing for, working in, and recovering from "the field."

Overseas Research: A Practical Guide is the first book designed explicitly to prepare scholars and professionals for the real-life challenges of living and working abroad. Opening with a discussion of site selection and project funding, the authors advise researchers on preparing for departure, setting up residence in the field, conducting research in an unfamiliar environment, employing field assistants, and organizing for and adjusting to the return home. The text is supplemented with insights, anecdotes, and tips from more than sixty scholars in a wide variety of disciplines, who conducted research in more than forty countries.

Christopher B. Barrett has conducted research in a dozen countries on four continents. He is currently assistant professor of economics at Utah State University. **Jeffrey W. Cason** has done extensive research in Latin America over the past ten years. He is currently assistant professor of political science at Middlebury College.

The Johns Hopkins University Press
BALTIMORE AND LONDON

ISBN 0-8018-5514-4

COVER DESIGN: MARTHA FARLOW